Theory for Theatre Studies: Memory

Theory for Theatre Studies meets the need for accessible, mid-length volumes that unpack keywords that lie at the core of the discipline. Aimed primarily at undergraduate students and secondarily at postgraduates and researchers, the volumes feature both background material historicizing the term and original, forward-looking research into intersecting theoretical trends in the field. Case studies ground volumes in praxis, and additional resources online ensure readers are equipped with the necessary skills and understanding as they move deeper into the discipline.

SERIES EDITORS

Susan Bennett, University of Calgary, Canada

Kim Solga, Western University, Canada

Published titles
Theory for Theatre Studies: Space
Kim Solga
Theory for Theatre Studies: Sound
Susan Bennett

Forthcoming titles
Theory for Theatre Studies: Bodies Soyica Diggs Colbert
Theory for Theatre Studies: Movement Rachel Fensham
Theory for Theatre Studies: Emotion Peta Tait
Theory for Theatre Studies: Economics Michael McKinnie
Theory for Theatre Studies: Aesthetics John Lutterbie

Theory for Theatre Studies: Memory

Milija Gluhovic

Series editors: Susan Bennett and Kim Solga

methuen | drama

LONDON · NEW YORK · OXFORD · NEW DELHI · SYDNEY

METHUEN DRAMA
Bloomsbury Publishing Plc
50 Bedford Square, London, WC1B 3DP, UK
1385 Broadway, New York, NY 10018, USA
29 Earlsfort Terrace, Dublin 2, Ireland

BLOOMSBURY, METHUEN DRAMA and the Methuen Drama logo are
trademarks of Bloomsbury Publishing Plc

First published in Great Britain 2020
Reprinted 2022

Series design by Louise Dugdale
Cover image © Henrik Sorensen / Getty Images

A catalogue record for this book is available from the British Library.

A catalog record for this book is available from the Library of Congress.

ISBN: HB: 978-1-4742-4665-1
         PB: 978-1-4742-4667-5
         ePDF: 978-1-4742-4664-4
         eBook: 978-1-4742-4668-2

Series: Theory for Theatre Studies

Typeset by Integra Software Services Pvt. Ltd.
Printed and bound in Great Britain

To find out more about our authors and books visit www.bloomsbury.com
and sign up for our newsletters.

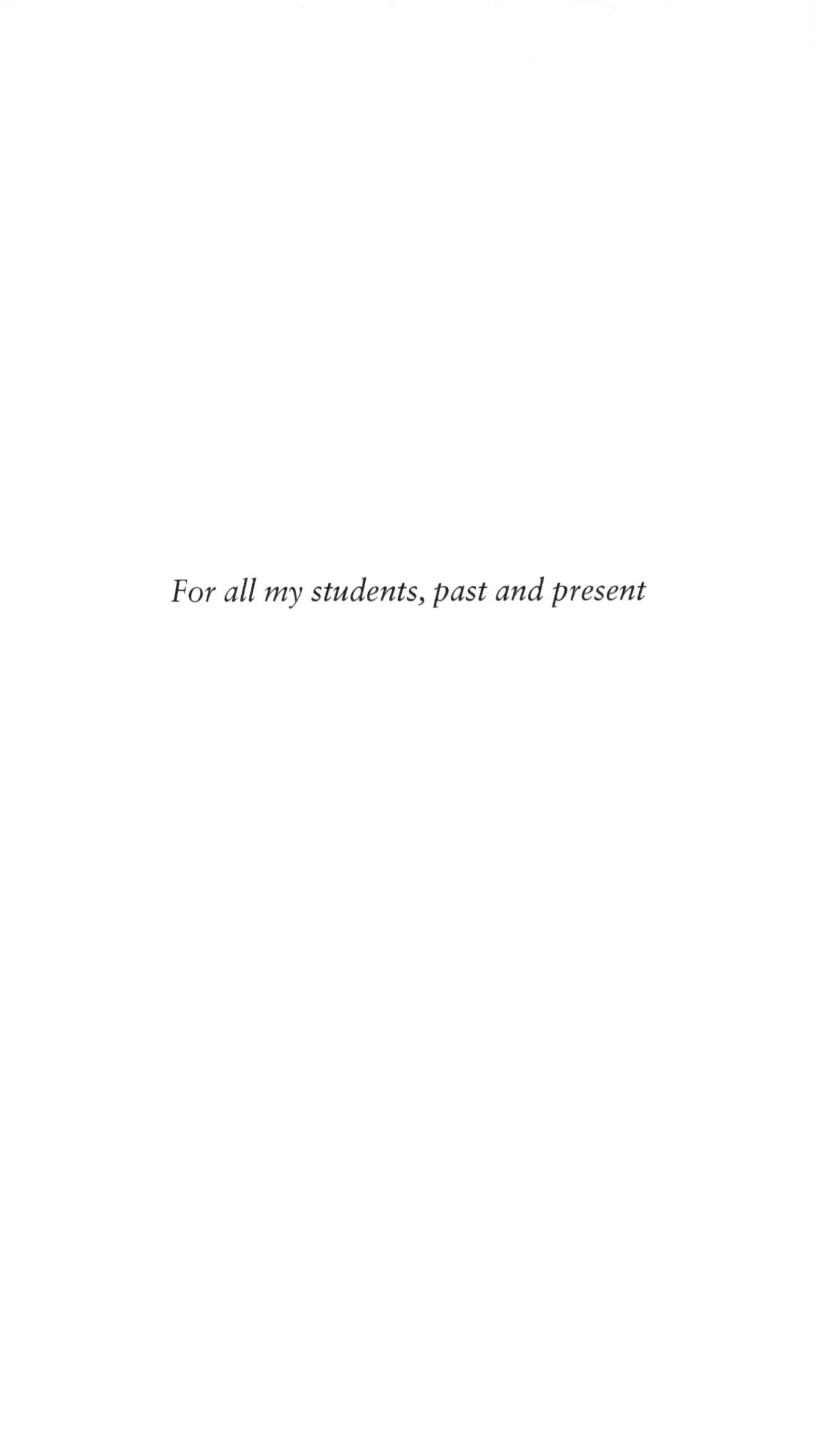

For all my students, past and present

CONTENTS

SERIES PREFACE

Theory for Theatre Studies (TfTS) is a series of introductory theoretical monographs intended for both undergraduate and postgraduate students as well as researchers branching out into fresh fields. It aims to introduce constellations of ideas, methods, theories, and rubrics central to the working concerns of scholars in theatre and performance studies at the opening of the twenty-first century. With a primary focus on twentieth-century developments, TfTS volumes offer accessible and provocative engagements with critical theory that inspire new ways of thinking theory in important disciplinary and interdisciplinary modes.

The series features full-length volumes explicitly aimed at unpacking sets of ideas that have coalesced around carefully chosen key terms in theatre and performance, such as space, sound, bodies, memory, movement, economies, and emotion. TfTS volumes do not aggregate existing essays, but rather provide a careful, fresh synthesis of what extensive reading by our authors reveals to be key nodes of interconnection between related theoretical models. The goal of these texts is to introduce readers to a wide variety of critical approaches and to unpack the complex theory useful for both performance analysis and creation.

Each volume in the series focuses on one specific set of theoretical concerns, constellated around a term that has become central to understanding the social and political labour of theatre and performance work at the turn of the millennium. The organization of each book follows a common template: Section One includes a historical overview of interconnected theoretical models, Section Two features extended case studies using twentieth- and twenty-first-century performances, and

Section Three looks ahead, as our authors explore important new developments in their constellation. Each volume is broad enough in scope to look laterally across its topic for compelling connections to related concerns, yet specific enough to be comprehensive in its assessment of its particular term. The ideas explored and explained through lively and detailed case studies provide diverse critical approaches for reading all kinds of plays and performances as well as starting points for practical exploration.

Each book includes a further reading section, and features a companion website with chapter summaries, questions for discussion, and a host of video and other web links.

Susan Bennett (University of Calgary, Canada)
and Kim Solga (Western University, Canada)

ACKNOWLEDGEMENTS

I would like to thank series editors Susan Bennett and Kim Solga for commissioning this book and for seeing it through to publication, along with Mark Dudgeon and Lara Bateman at Bloomsbury. Thanks also to the anonymous readers for the advice. Thanks to André Amálio, Lola Arias, and colleagues at the Maxim Gorki Theatre the Schaubühne am Lehniner Platz in Berlin for sharing their archives so generously. Thanks to Maria Delgado, Emine Fişek, Karen Fricker, Helen Gilbert, Jean Graham-Jones, Anna Hájková, and Katrin Sieg for sharing work in progress with me as I worked on the final parts of this book. Colleagues and students at the University of Warwick deserve a mention for engaging with this research in various ways and at different stages. I am especially grateful to my one-time mentor at the University of Toronto, Tamara Trojanowska, and the late Ross Chambers from the University of Michigan, who was the first to introduce me to testimonial writing through his guest course at the University of British Columbia (UBC). Thanks to the University of Warwick for the sabbatical leave on which, in apart, I wrote this text and for research support in the final stages of its preparation. I am particularly grateful to Agnieszka Polakowska, for reading the manuscript and commenting extensively, and my research assistants Theo Aiolfi and Eliza Tivadar, for helping with manuscript preparation. Love and thanks to Agnieszka, Ameet, Anuradha, Bishnupriya, Bobby, Emine, Janelle, Katrin, Kim, Maria, Nataša, Neso, Nobuko, Olivera, Shirin, and Silvija for their friendship during and beyond this project. To my family, thank you for your steadfast and loving support.

Introduction

In Walter Benjamin's famous essay 'On the Concept of History', written by the German-Jewish philosopher in the midst of the Second World War, we find the following assertion: 'Articulating the past historically does not mean recognizing it "the way it really was." It means appropriating a memory as it flashes up in a moment of danger. Historical materialism wishes to hold fast that image of the past which unexpectedly appears to the historical subject in a moment of danger' (2006 [1940]: 391–2). His claim still resonates powerfully for many today, at the end of the second decade of the twenty-first century. For Benjamin, memory is the central category of historical consciousness. The philosopher offers a view of a historical/redemptive methodology founded on gathering and working with fragments of the past as they break through into our present, where they become provisionally available. Benjamin admonishes the historicist for seeking to immobilize and hold on to the past in the form of a genuine and unchanging historical image. He calls on us to seize hold of elusive histories that have been obscured by insistence on history's 'genuine' image, not in order to fix also those histories and establish new genuine images, or new eternal truths, but rather to allow the past, repressed, and often marginalized, to step into the light of a present moment of danger and reorient its politics towards a more just future.

The historical context for Benjamin's reflections makes it easy to identify both the moment of danger that he refers to, namely the rise of fascism and Nazism, and the memory in question: 'of history's vanquished "enslaved ancestors"' (Levi and Rothberg 2018: 355). As I write this introduction, in 2019, the moment of danger is that of hard-right forces that have surged to power in liberal democracies across the globe, and the memory that flashes up is that of fascism itself. To borrow from Wendy Brown's opening paragraph in *On the Ruins of Neoliberalism*:

> Every election brings a new shock: neo-Nazis in the German parliament, neofascists in the Italian one, Brexit ushered in by tabloid-fuelled xenophobia, the rise of white nationalism in Scandinavia, authoritarian regimes taking shape in Turkey and Eastern Europe, and of course, Trumpism. Racist, anti-Islamic, and anti-Semitic hatefulness and bellicosity grow in the streets and across the internet, and newly coalesced far-right groups have burst boldly into the public light after years of lurking mostly in the shadows. (2019: 1)

Since Brown wrote this assessment, the re-election of Narendra Modi in India and the election of Boris Johnson as British prime minister have only intensified this predicament.

As Levi and Rothberg argue:

> For Benjamin, the question of whether the historical subject could indeed appropriate that memory as it flashed up meant wondering whether the historical subject could direct its hatred at its real oppressors and sacrifice itself for the right cause, or if its capacity to do so had been so atrophied that all the historical resources that could constitute a tradition of the oppressed had fallen into fascist hands. (2018: 355)

This is no longer the case, however, as the authors point out, for the notion of the historical subject has become much less stable over the course of the twentieth, and now the twenty-first, century. The questions we are facing today concern our memory of fascism: what it actually consists of, what its appropriation may mean or involve, and whether it would prove enlightening or distracting in the context of our present-day realities.

The contemporary public sphere is dominated by memories of wars and genocides, with the Holocaust foremost among them. In *Left-Wing Melancholia: Marxism, History, and Memory*, a complex and compelling account of contemporary political culture, Enzo Traverso argues that, beginning in the 1980s, the rise of memory and memorialization as a cultural fetish coincided with the defeat of state socialism, producing what he calls a 'mutilated dialectic' that takes us into a present weighed down by memories of the past and completely unable to project a future (2016: 9).[1] According to Traverso, it is the absence of utopias in the modern world that propels our obsession with the past, while our relatively uneventful transition into the twenty-first century means that nothing has supplanted the horrors of war, genocide, and the camps in our memory (2016: 9). Following his argument, the focus on victims in our view of history has greatly impacted the means of engaging with the collective past: 'The memory of the Gulag erased that of revolution, the memory of the Holocaust replaced that of antifascism, and the memory of slavery eclipsed that of anticolonialism: the remembrance of the victims seems unable to coexist with the recollection of their hopes, of their struggles, of their conquests and their defeats' (2016: 10). Liberal humanitarianism thus sacralizes the victim but neglects the vanquished and is the opposite of left-wing commitment – a pre-emptive strike against political change even before its inevitable co-option into imperialist ideology.

Traverso's version of left-wing melancholy, in contrast, has an affirmative dimension, or what might be described as the minimal expression of revolutionary potential. 'This melancholia', he says, 'does not mean a retreat into a closed universe of suffering and remembering; it is rather a constellation of emotions and feelings that envelop a historical transition, the only way in which the search for new ideas and projects can coexist with the sorrow and mourning for a lost realm of revolutionary experiences' (2016: xiv). This affirmation does not signal some rarefied aristocratic contemplation but rather an experiential response to an objective crisis at the level of political history. Traverso's stated intention is to distil something forward-facing and catalytic from the apparent defeats of left-wing ideology and from their remembrance: left-wing melancholia 'perceives the tragedies and the lost battles of the past as a burden and debt, which are also a promise of redemption' (2016: xv).

Traverso's latest book, *The New Faces of Fascism: Populism and the Far Right*, continues these reflections, positing the Holocaust in particular as an object of our obsessive focus to examine how its memory has been institutionalized by governments, ritualized by official commemorations, and reified by the culture industry despite the weakening of its pedagogical and cohesive role on the contemporary geopolitical stage. The Jews who were the victims of genocide during the Second World War are now implicated in the oppression that their nation state of Israel, as a result of its foundations, is seen as perpetrating upon the Palestinian people. As Traverso observes, 'It is worth getting a proper measure of the perverse consequences of a politics of memory that makes the Jews into the paradigmatic victim and, at the same time, silences or trivialises the memory of the victims of colonial violence' (2019: 59–60).

While the Holocaust made the Zionist project of founding a new state in which Jews could live free and protected lives a matter of utmost urgency and importance, the creation of the state of Israel came at a great cost. The war of 1948 was a war of liberation and triumph for Jews and Israelis while also being an experience of defeat, forced expulsion, material loss, and ongoing trauma for the Palestinians. As Elias Khoury writes, 'The everyday reality of life in Palestine clearly indicates that the 1948 war was merely the beginning of the catastrophic event. It did not end when the cease-fire agreements of 1949 were signed. In fact, 1948 was the beginning of a phenomenon that continues to this day' (2018: xiii). Among the Palestinians, this catastrophe – the Nakba, as it is referred to – has become 'the key site of (their) collective memory and national identity' (Abu-Lughod and Sa'di 2007: 4). More than an individual and a collective memory orally transmitted across generations, it is 'reckoned as the beginning of contemporary Palestinian history, a history of catastrophic changes, violent repression, and refusal to disappear' (Abu-Lughod and Sa'di 2007: 5).

The daunting and complex task of acknowledging the Palestinians' tragedy and including it in Israeli memory explains why the Israelis have chosen the alternative of forgetting instead. Michael Confino describes the inexorable dialectic between forgetting and remembering that makes the daily repression of the memory of the Nakba conditional on it being brought back, again and again, into Israeli consciousness: 'The Nakba is part of their history, and an important part: they remember the Nakba whether they deny it or relate it in prose or in poetry. The very attempt to erase the memory of the Nakba is the outcome of an immense mobilization of political, economic, and cultural effort' (Confino 2016: n.p.).

I was struck by the silencing and erasure of this memory during the Eurovision Song Contest held in Tel Aviv under the slogan 'Dare to Dream' in May 2019. The event was meant to symbolize inclusion, diversity, and unity to resonate with the core values of the Eurovision Song Contest. As Karen Fricker and I have argued elsewhere, the contest serves as an arena in which both the national and the European identities of participating nations are confirmed and where the cultural struggles over the meanings, frontiers, and limits of Europe are enacted (2013: 3). Its 2019 edition was particularly telling in this regard, having been held on 18 May, almost a year to the day since the commencement of the Great March of the Return protests along the Gaza border and only a few days after Israel's Independence Day on 15 May.

The speech given by Tel Aviv's Mayor Ron Huldai during an important Eurovision milestone (The Semi-Final Allocation

Draw and Host City Insignia Exchange) lays out the rationale behind the chosen 'Dare to Dream' motif:

> From its beginning, this city [of Tel Aviv] belongs to dreamers who never give up. 110 years ago, the dreamers built a city of modernism in the middle of the sand dunes. Today it is one of the most energetic cities. The dreamers of Tel Aviv built a city of technology, in a place that has no resources. Tel Aviv is the start-up city of the start-up nation; we have the highest concentration of start-up companies in the world. The dreamers of Tel Aviv built a city based on the values of tolerance, freedom and human rights, which accepts everyone and is open to the world. (transcript of speech at Eurovision Song Contest 2018)

This message obscures the fact that the city holds within it a number of sites that were Arab villages until the outbreak of the War of Independence, a trend of Palestinian dispossession that is ongoing as large-scale urban construction projects in Tel Aviv continue at the cost of destroying their former homes (see Assmann 2018).

Watching the Eurovision spectacle, it was hard not to see the disconnect between this cultural performance and the contemporary geopolitics of colonialism, occupation, and warfare in the region. An emotional performance during the second semi-final by the Shalva Band, whose members all live with disabilities, brought this into sharp relief. Their song, entitled 'A Million Dreams', earned widespread praise from viewers in both Israel and abroad for its message of inclusivity and acceptance. The Eurovision organization praised the band for 'inspiring us to think differently about challenges and acceptance', while many viewers in Israel said the performance brought them to tears (Staff 2019: n.p.). As the group received a long-standing ovation at the end of their act and the contest's host Bar Refaeli commented on the performance while holding back tears, I was struck by the discord between this state-sanctioned display of disability empowerment and Israel's use of maiming as a deliberate biopolitical tactic in its occupation of Palestine, with the latter being especially manifest during Operation Protective Edge, the fifty-one days during the summer of 2014 when medical personnel in both Gaza and the West Bank reported mounting evidence of 'shoot to cripple' practices in the Israeli Defence Forces (IDF).

Jasbir Puar has written at some length about what she calls 'the right to maim', meaning the extension of the 'right to kill' claimed by states at war through reliance on practices that cripple civilians and communities while avoiding fatalities, for example by using bullets that fragment and splinter bones and targeting crucial civilian infrastructure along with medical services and providers (see Puar 2015a: 218–19; also Puar 2017). As she states: 'Maiming as intentional practice expands biopolitics beyond simply the question of "right of death and power over life;" maiming becomes a primary vector by which biopolitical control is operated in colonized space, modulating not only the folding between life and death but also human and inhuman' (2015a: 219).[2] A statement from Maher Najjar, the deputy general of Gaza's Coastal Municipalities Water Utilities (CMWU) during the 2014 operation, clearly points to the proximity of death and debilitation:

> There is no water reaching any of the houses right now. We're facing a real catastrophe. Sewage pumps cannot work because the power plant has been destroyed, so we have sewage flooding the streets of Gaza. We can't assess the extent of damage as we can't even go out without risking our lives right now... We have the total collapse of all essential services and there's nothing we can do about it. Believe me, it would be better if the Israelis just dropped the nuclear bomb on Gaza and get done with it. This is the worst ever assault on the Gaza Strip. (Cited in Puar 2015b: 9)

Puar's focus on maiming as an effective means of depopulating territories while seemingly avoiding casualties shines a light on realities that usually remains ignored and literally unseen, as they had been during Israel's 'Dare to Dream' edition of the Eurovision. As Brown's insightful snapshot of the current international political situation also reveals, we are living in a world that is so riddled with hidden dangers and antagonisms as to give new urgency to Benjamin's reflections on the role of memory in times of historical crisis. As Janelle Reinelt observes, 'political activism seems not only urgent but mandatory to a degree that harkens back to an earlier period of global political activity in the 1960s and 1970s' (forthcoming), adding also that '[i]t is hard to remember, much less embrace, previous theorizations of a postpolitical consensus that flattened debate and consolidated the state' (forthcoming).

What kinds of responses are open to those attuned to and apprehensive about recent shifts in the global sociopolitical landscape and what can memory bring to the process? When posing this question in the context of theatre studies, we quickly arrive at performance, as Reinelt points out: 'In the years since 2016 we have seen an outpouring of reconsiderations of the relationship between politics and performance, a focus on specific global problems such as migration and global warming, and a new (or at least renewed) respect for artistic activism generated by theatre and performance artists' (forthcoming). It is thus the intersections between contemporary theatre and performance, the interdisciplinary field of memory studies, and the global politics of memory that constitute the focus of this volume in the Theory for Theatre Studies series.

In the rest of this Introduction, I want to turn to the work of two theatre and performance studies scholars, Marvin Carlson and Rebecca Schneider, whose concerns are broadly relevant for the subject of my analysis; in particular, their theories of theatre and performance which recognize memory, in all its diverse, heterogeneous strands, as a vital resource for political critique that orients our expectations and might guide our actions in our moment of danger.

Using different forms of storytelling to communicate the past has always been a way for communities to educate and entertain themselves, to guide their future and remember their past behaviour – a means of keeping culture in lively negotiation. Theatre, as Marvin Carlson suggests in *The Haunted Stage: The Theatre as Memory Machine*, is particularly well-suited to this multi-layered communicative task, since all plays and performances, no matter how new or original they may be, have embedded within them aspects of our individual and cultural memories:

> The retelling of stories already told, the re-enactment of events already enacted, the reexperience of emotions already experienced, these are and have always been the central concerns of theatre in all times and places, but closely allied to these concerns are the particular production dynamics of theatre: the stories it chooses to tell, the bodies and other physical materials it utilizes to tell them, and the places in which they are told. Each of these production elements are ... also, to a striking degree, composed of material 'that we have seen before,' and the memory of that recycled material as it moves through new and different productions contributes in no small measure to the richness and density of the operations of theatre in general as a site of memory, both personal and cultural. (2003: 3–4)

Carlson's vision of the theatre's close relation to memory can be usefully placed next to Rebecca Schneider's recent writings on how gesture (as it is understood in theatre and performance studies) confirms, by its re-iterative form, that 'the past may yet have another future' (2018: 288). Schneider had rigorously investigated the aesthetic and political potential of re-enactments already in *Performing Remains* (2011), passionately arguing that performance can be engaged as what remains, rather than what disappears. As she explains, re-enactment refers to a wide range of forms and practices of which historical re-enactments in living history museums, historical reality television shows, and preservation societies are only some examples. 'In many ways', writes Schneider, 'reenactment has become the popular and practice-based wing of what has been called the twentieth-century academic "memory industry"' (2011: 2). A wide range of re-enactment types are present in art and performance, exhibiting a variety of aesthetic and political goals and engaging their audiences in many different ways. One approach is to restage artworks and historically significant events as precisely as possible. Schneider offers as examples the Wooster Group's recreation of Grotowski's *Akropolis* here, and Rod Dickinson's repetition of Dr Stanley Milgram's infamous 1961 social psychology experiment 'Obedience to Authority'. The experiment was itself partially inspired by the 1961 trial of Adolf Eichmann and tested how far participants would go to obey an authoritative scientist in inflicting pain on another. Precision is not a necessity of re-enactments, however: Jeremy Deller's *The Battle of Orgreave* reconstructs a confrontation between striking British coal miners and the police from 1981 while also taking artistic liberties and departing from the event's established account.

Reflecting on the popular appeal of Civil War re-enactments in the United States, Schneider identifies affective engagement ('the *feel*') as a crucial component of their resonance (2011: 50). The re-enactors that she interviewed and observed sought authenticity from the experience, a means of feeling the event's impact directly, on their own skin, in a way that escapes more mediated forms of historical representation, such as written accounts, photos, or film. In other words, these people 'wanted to *experience it for themselves* and add to their historical acumen by way of their own physical engagement' (Schneider 2011: 54; original emphasis). This kind of 'communing with' the spectre of the past is not without its moral dilemmas and difficulties, especially in societies that are still haunted by their difficult histories. 'No one has ever worked through an injury without repeating it', Judith Butler reminds us: 'There is no possibility of not repeating. The only question that remains is: How will that repetition occur, at what site ... and with what pain and promise?' (1997b: 102).

In the essay 'That the Past May Yet Have Another Future: Gesture in the Times of Hands Up', Schneider imagines a relationship to the past that serves as a basis for addressing contemporary wounds. Her reflections are prompted by recent acts of racial violence in the United States, and more specifically the police killing of Eric Garner on Staten Island in New York City on 17 July 2014, and that of Michael Brown in Ferguson, Missouri, on 9 August 2014. She begins by restating a claim made by Thomas DeFrantz and Gustavo Furtado: 'Reenactments are, above all, disturbances to the perceived linearity of time. Through corporeal repetition the past gains a ghostly simultaneity with the present, and every repetition harbours the possibility of difference – that is, the possibility that the past may yet have another future' (qtd. in Schneider 2018: 288). In responding to it, Schneider turns to an array of gestures, from Paleolithic negative hand stencils in France to the Hands Up protest gesture of the Black Lives Matter movement across the contemporary United States, in order to think through how they – and we – address the urgencies of racial violence (alongside the urgencies of climate change). Conceptualizing gesture as engaged in a dynamics of call and response, she asks whether there is a time limit on response-ability: 'When rituals of interpellative violence recur again and again across (black) bodies "without any succession," as Althusser writes, and when police gestures carry the ongoing afterlives of slavery in forms of police brutality "in the wake" of the middle passage, as Christina Sharpe writes, are we not engaged antiphonically with the past at every re-irruption?' (2018: 287).

Reflecting on the 'Hands up, don't shoot!' protest action, she argues that the 'gesture of two hands up holds and moves, in syncopated time, both response and call' (2018: 297). For Schneider, our understanding of the relation between past and present is the product of a politics of our time: social practices that create different regimes of historicity, different relations between past, present, and future. Analysing the impact of the 'hands-up' gesture, she notes: 'Both response and call, the gesture moved beyond the events in New York and Ferguson to all sides and called on others to respond in kind in an effort to move the ongoing "afterlife of slavery," the ongoing historical drama of police brutality against black people, toward a future otherwise' (2018: 297). Schneider's account of the 'irrevocable' nature of certain violent histories – histories that remain unresolved and thus trouble the distinction between a fully 'absent' past and a fully 'present' present – influences my approach to memory and performance. Theatre, in its engagement with memory in and through performance, makes clear that repair requires repositioning the body not only discursively but also spatially and interpersonally.

Schneider's reflections on the ongoing, uneven, and destabilizing intrusion of irrevocable pasts into an unredeemed present – and the entanglement of the synchronic and diachronic that follows from them – nowhere more visible than in the differential vulnerability of racialized subjects such Eric Garner and Michael Brown, as well as Carlson's vision, rooted in the phenomenological terrain of the theatre, that shows the ways in which art reconstructs worlds by taking hold of the past illustrate leading examples of how theatre and performance studies scholars have theorised the power of performance over the years, offering new approaches and new paradigms of thinking, making, and acting. In the context of the global resurgence of far-right authoritarianism, white nationalism, and neofascism, it is important to ask whether performance can continue to act as conduit between the past and the present in a way that opens new lines of sight. Why does memory hold such a privileged place in contemporary experience? How has it become such an important political tool in response to the challenges of modernity? And how can the discipline of theatre studies define and deploy this term, theoretically and in practice?

These are some of the questions engaged in the present volume of *Theory for Theatre Studies: Memory*, which is itself organized into three sections. The first section lays out the theoretical foundations for the study of memory today, referencing such seminal figures and theorist in the field as Sigmund Freud, Tadeusz Kantor, Cathy Caruth, Marianne Hirsch, and Susannah Radstone. It also provides a brief discussion of classical and medieval studies of mnemotechnica to place the recent 'memory boom' in a broader context and draws on the vivid example of Tadeusz Kantor's *Wielopole, Wielopole* (1980) to demonstrate the impact of memory discourse on modernist and neo-avant-garde theatre and performance.

Building on the theoretical framework established in Section One, Section Two uses three key case studies to illustrate some of the ways that theatre artists in the twenty-first century have grappled with the pressing issues at stake in memory studies, including questions of truth and authenticity, debates about the ethics and politics of memory, and the inescapable tension between memory and history. I start by asking whether performing memory and history can be reparatory and then go on to reflect on contestations over memory and the significance of the emergence of reparations as a key term with which to think about the wrongs of the past and the possibilities of repair. Then I move to the works selected for analysis – Lola Arias's *Minefield/Campo minado* (UK/Argentina 2016), Yael Ronen's *Common Ground* (Germany/Bosnia and Herzegovina 2014), and Robert Lepage's *The Seven Streams of the River Ota* (Canada 1994–8) – that speak to the global currency of memory in theatre today when considered individually, and only more so when placed side-by-side. In examining the aesthetics, ethics, and politics of these works, Section Two thus aims to identify some of the strategies that theatre artists have recently used to explore memories of war, conflict, and contested pasts.

Of particular interest in this section will be the interplay between repetition and immediacy, and between theatricality and performativity, that is key to these case studies, as well as recent debates on oral history and testimony (Radstone, Taylor, Stauffer, Chambers) and historical re-enactment and delegated performance (Schneider, Bishop). In the context of neoliberal policies, a lack of institutional justice, and multiple lapses on the part of human beings and political institutions that, in failing to listen well to survivors, deny them redress by negating their testimony and thwarting their claims for justice, these performances foreground difficult truths about the desire and the potential for political forgiveness, transitional justice, and political reconciliation. In the face of trauma, they neither give us justice nor assert the redemptive value of bearing witness. Instead, they make us acknowledge that which can never leave us. These performances engage the work of mourning in order not to disavow the past; they constantly demand that both their producers and their audiences work their own lifelines into recent history to connect the past with the present and the future. As I argue in this section of the book, they may also help us to negotiate and re-imagine our contemporary moment of endless war and develop a different attitude towards life and death.

The third section of this volume, entitled 'Memory and Migration', looks at the problematics of memory in a global context by exploring the subject of migration/immigration that has become a major divisive issue of the twenty-first century. In their book *Memory in a Global Age* (2010), Aleida Assmann and Sebastian Conrad state: 'Until recently, the dynamics of memory production unfolded primarily within the bounds of the nation state ... Today, memory and the global have to be studied together, as it has become impossible to understand the trajectories of memory outside a global frame of reference' (2). In this context, collectively experienced catastrophes such as slavery, the Holocaust, the Gulags and other atrocities, ecological disasters, famine, and forced migrations 'emerg[e] as privileged issues in a politics of global accountability' (7). Section Three thus discusses the politics of remembering and forgetting in relation to two case studies that explore the subject of migration and memory in relation to the European colonial past and intercontinental migration.

First, I discuss the National Theatre production of *Small Island* (London, UK, 2019), adapted by Helen Edmondson from Andrea Levy's novel, which explores the history of the

Windrush generation in the UK. For those who were colonized, questions of identity and belonging were a key legacy of empire. However, it was the 1948 Nationality Act, which granted free movement to Commonwealth citizens, which provoked large-scale West Indian migration to Great Britain. 'In the 1960s, when the children of the Windrush generation were arriving with their parents', writes Catherine Hall, 'there were no issues with their entry to the "mother country": they were travelling internally within the empire. They were registered as "freely landed": that was the wording on the landing cards destroyed by the Home Office in 2010' (2020: 11). Through my discussion of *Small Island*, I revisit the history of the Windrush generation in the UK in relation to the Windrush scandal (2018–), reflecting on some of the ways in which the histories of race and slavery have figured in the recent past in Britain. Then I turn to André Amálio's *Portugal Is Not a Small Country* in order to address the contested terrain of Portugal's colonial history and migrations. By exploring the continuities between the racisms of the past and the present, the performance addresses histories of the enslaved and their survival, of the perpetrators and the beneficiaries, thus linking this historical trauma and loss to hopes for reconciliation, the repair of relations damaged by historical injustice.

Building on insights from the previous two sections that suggest that memory in the twenty-first century must be studied from a transnational, transcultural, and global perspective (Rothberg 2009; Assmann and Conrad 2010), Section Three also explores the possibility of an advent of a new, fourth phase in memory studies – and of its implications for the study of theatre and performance today – which we are witnessing in consequence of our growing consciousness of the Anthropocene and which takes the gradual scalar expansion characterizing the previous phases to a new level.

SECTION ONE

Mapping Memory:
Theorizing Recollection

The concept of memory is complex and seldom invoked in precisely the same sense, hence the ramifications, traditions, and histories, which are conflated in their current usages, need to be unpacked and evaluated. In this introduction, I thus discuss three aspects of memory discourse: the historical (relation between historiography and individual/collective memory), psychological (trauma, mourning, and melancholia), and philosophical (subjectivity), as well as how they can be brought to bear on my subsequent discussion of different layers of theatrical imagination.

The Classical and Medieval Practice
of Mnemotechnics: How Memory
Works on Stage

In this section, I begin by discussing the classical practice of mnemotechnics, the prized art of memory. The invention of mnemotechnics (the *ars memoriae*) is credited to the Greek poet Simonides of Keos (sixth century BCE). In Quintilian's version of the legend:

> [Simonides] had written an ode of the kind that was usually composed in honour of victorious athletes, to celebrate the achievement of one who had gained the crown for boxing. Part of the sum for which he had contracted was refused him on the ground that, following the common practice of poets, he had introduced a digression in praise of Castor and Pollux, and he was told that, in view of what he had done, he had best ask for the rest of the sum due from those whose deeds he had extolled. And according to the story they paid their debt. For when a great banquet was given in honour of the boxer's success, Simonides was summoned forth from the feast, to which he had been invited, by a message to the effect that two youths who had ridden to the door urgently desired his presence. He found no trace of them, but what followed proved to him that the gods have shown their gratitude. For he had scarcely crossed the threshold on his way out, when the banqueting hall fell in upon the heads of the guests and wrought such havoc among them that the relatives of the dead who came to seek the bodies for burial were unable to distinguish not merely the faces but even the limbs of the dead. Then it is said, Simonides, who remembered the order in which the guests had been sitting, succeeded in restoring to each man his own dead.
>
> (Quintilian 1980: 11–13)

According to the *Simonides* legend, the first memory theatre consists of mutilated corpses: 'The finding of absent images heals what has been destroyed: the art of memoria restores shape to the mutilated victims and makes them recognisable by establishing their place and seat in life … A survivor – the poet as a bearer of cultural memory – is necessary to inscribe the representatives of the unrecognisable, absent primary signs in the syntax of place' (Lachmann 1997: 6, 9). Only after they have been linked with the place where they sat do they become identifiable and regain their names, through a second act of naming, an act of memory. Quintilian's narrative suggests that this process of identifying through naming should be understood as a vicarious supplying of images.

At the beginning of memoria as art, therefore, stands the effort to technologize the work of mourning. The recollection of order mobilizes a work of reconstruction to counter the destruction, even as this destruction marks the beginning of re-membering. In addition, as Jody Enders points out in her study *The Medieval Theater of Cruelty*, the *Simonides* legend problematizes some key dramatic features of mnemotechnics: 'that the object of remembrance must first die in order to be brought back to life; that the metaphorically encrypted and subsequently resurrected dead are moving, talking images or simulacra; that mnemotechnics renders present those who are absent or dead; and that it does so by repainting their picture and by giving them voice' (Enders 1999: 72). As we shall see, the authentic act of remembering, which closes the drama of the catastrophe and opens that of the burial, 'inaugurates a commemorative model that establishes fascinating parallels between theatre and birth, death, and resurrection' (Enders 1999: 72) – a model echoed by Tadeusz Kantor's 'Theatre of Death'.[1]

Tadeusz Kantor (1915–90) is one of Poland's foremost theatre artists of the second half of the twentieth century, whose work left a deep imprint on the theatre and performance arts in Europe and around the world. Kantor studied at the Academy of Fine Arts in Kraków, where his work as a painter and stage designer evolved in a constant dialogue with the dominant avant-garde movements such as constructivism, dadaism, and surrealism in the 1920s and 1930s. He survived the Second World War working as a decoration painter in the Słowacki Theatre in Kraków. During the war he also engaged in clandestine theatre activities, famously staging Juliusz Słowacki's *Balladyna* (1839) and Stanisław

Wyspiański's *The Return of Odysseus* (*Powrót Odysa* 1907), the latter of which he would revisit towards the end of his career. Together with his Cricot 2 theatre company, founded in 1955, he presented many radical stagings of Stanisław Ignacy Witkiewicz (1885–1939, pen name Witkacy), which brought these works much critical acclaim at theatre festivals in France, Italy, and the UK in the late 1960s and early 1970s.

In the mid-1970s, however, Kantor moved into a new territory: the cycle of performances that he entitled the 'Theatre of Death' (1975–90) marked the beginning of his sustained, almost obsessive engagement with historical trauma, memory, and forgetting. For Kantor, who can be seen as one of the most significant figures among the many Polish artists and scholars who have tried to engage the traumatic experiences of the twentieth century, especially the Holocaust, the stakes of memory are enormous. His memory-theatre constitutes a platform of interventionist cultural and political engagement, a form of repair and redress. Having directly experienced the Holocaust and the Second World War in Poland, he sought to represent and commemorate those staggering losses in the hope of a better future. Keenly aware of power as a central factor in mediating the public appearance of collective memories in communist Poland, in his performances, Kantor constantly challenged the frames of intelligibility. That is, concerned with epistemological and ontological problems that were more than incidental, he exposed and critiqued the dominant structures of recognition and knowledge that shaped the representation of the Second World War in the communist East of Europe, circumscribed the war's meaning, and effaced violence's affect – certain forms of grief and mourning that could not be openly expressed in Poland of the day. In so doing, he allowed for heretofore silenced, suppressed, and disavowed experiences of his audiences to emerge. Challenging their historical imagination of the two world wars, his performances aimed at renewing his audiences' affective engagement with the dark sides of Europe's past.

Wielopole, Wielopole, the second production from his 'Theatre of Death' developed in Florence in 1980, got its title after a small town near Kraków where Kantor was born. 'In the square', remembers Kantor,

> stood a chapel with some sort of saint for the Catholic faithful. In the same square was a well near which Jewish weddings were held, primarily when the moon was full. On one side stood the church, the rectory, and the Catholic cemetery, and on the other the synagogue, the narrow Jewish lanes, and another cemetery, somewhat different. Both sides existed in a harmonious symbiosis. (Kantor cited in Pleśniarowicz 2004: 11)

As Kantor further relates on another occasion, 'During the last war half of the town was destroyed, many houses were burnt down and the Jews deported' (Kantor cited in Thibaudat 1990: 183–4).

Like in the Simonides legend, the performance of *Wielopole, Wielopole* also starts with an act of naming, through which Kantor introduces his dead relatives, the protagonists of this memory séance:

> Here is my Grandmother, my mother's mother, Katarzyna. And that's her brother, the Priest. Some used to call him uncle. He will die shortly. My father sits over there. The first from the left. On the reverse of this photograph he sends his greetings. Date: 12th September 1914. Mother Helka will be here any minute. The rest are Uncles and Aunts. They went the way of all flesh, somewhere in the world. Now they are in the room, imprinted as memories: Uncle Karol, Uncle Olek, Auntie Mańka, Auntie Józka. From this moment on, their fortunes begin to change passing through a series of radical alterations, often quite embarrassing, such as they would have been unable to face, had they been among the living. (Kantor 1990a: 17)

This act of naming the dead was absent from the beginning of this memory séance. Instead, the audience saw Kantor's solitary figure walking around the performance space as if in search for the remnants of his life. His were the first gestures of summoning up the memory of his childhood, gestures strongly reminiscent of the underlying principles of the ancient mnemonics. According to the ancients, the would-be memory artist remembered (or imagined) an organized space – houses or theatres were commonly suggested.[2] Within this space he distributed at regular intervals images that would serve as prompts to the memory. Later, when the user wished to remember something, he would, in an act of literal re-collection, mentally retrieve the images in any order he desired. In a similar vein, at the beginning of the séance, Kantor moved around the performance space – a simple wooden platform – empty except for a few pieces of furniture. He opened and closed the wardrobe, arranged the chairs, moved the bed with the mannequin of the priest on it out of the way. After this initial procedure of 'furnishing' the room of memory, a signal was given, and the sliding doors at the back of the room were opened. From this anteroom area of history, memory, and loss, two groups of actors appeared on stage: Kantor's family, whose bodies were scattered around, and a group of soldiers, who positioned themselves in a corner, as if posing for a camera.

The process of furnishing the room of memory was then continued by two identically looking stage figures: Kantor's uncles Karol and Olek, played by the Janicki twins. Through the stage presence of the twins, Kantor explicitly evoked the figure of doubling, which is the basic figure of the work of memory. As Renate Lachmann reminds us, the Simonides legend assigns a central role to the Dioscuri in the development of mnemotechnics:

> The twins who, as thanks for his song of praise, call Simonides outside across the threshold of the door and of time without revealing themselves to him, thereby saving

him from catastrophe, appear as the personification of doubling. Personification in absentia is already in itself a kind of doubling: those absent are represented by the meaning ascribed to them in the context of the legend. The twin gods present a *Doppelgänger* pair, each of whom undergoes a further doubling process: the boxer with his opponent (as in a duel), the horse tamer with his animal (suggesting the symbiosis of horse and rider). This prototypical duo, in acting out the *Doppelgänger* relations between mortal body and immortal soul, death and life, portrays synchronically the metamorphosis from life to death, a metamorphosis that takes place in the conclave following a temporal linearity, and in the course of which the corpses become the *Doppelgänger* of the banqueters. (Lachmann 1997: 8)

Immediately the twins in Kantor's performance recognized that everything on the stage was out of place. Since memories could not be induced or brought forth until things had been put in order, the uncles – following a lot of double talk – set to work. After moving things about in a slapstick manner, they finally agreed on the rightful places in which the body of the dead priest, the chairs, the window, and other pieces of furniture should be set. The performance got underway only after everything was satisfactorily put in place; a hymn played over the loudspeakers; and Grandma, who up until then has been lying on the floor in silence, got up to speak.

In *Wielopole, Wielopole*, memory is imaged as a room, which means memory is localized within a concrete, material form. Here, as in Samuel Beckett's *Krapp's Last Tape*, where it is imaged as a tape recorder, 'memory seems self-contained, redeemable, and very present, rather than diffuse and elusive'; it depends for its 'use' on a proper configuration of the mnemonic field that would in turn induce memories (Malkin 1999: 44). The theatricalization of memory function and human subjectivity in these two pieces highlights 'the dualism of rememberer and memory, where memory is imagined as objectified "other" that cannot be completely controlled'

(Malkin 1999: 44). Thus, both Kantor and Beckett present us 'not only with the act of remembering a life, but with a dialogue between living and remembrance, present and past: Man and his Memory' (Malkin 1999: 45). Clearly there are vestiges of ancient mnemotechnics at work in Kantor's *Wielopole, Wielopole*.

We are reminded of the rhetorical origins of Kantor's 'room of memory' even though Kantor does not explicitly acknowledge this. Ancient and medieval writers on memory recognized, as we do now, the dual aspects of storage and recollection involved in remembering. Their most common model for human memory likened it to a tablet or a parchment page upon which a person writes. Re-collection was essentially a task of composition, literally bringing together matters found in their various storage places, and re-assembling them in a new place. Furthermore, one of two major metaphors used in ancient and medieval times for the educated memory was that of thesaurus, 'storage-room', and later 'strong-box'. Whereas the metaphor of the seal-in-wax or written tablets was a model for the process of making the memorial phantasm and storing it in a place in memory, the storage-room metaphor refers both to the contents of such a memory and to its internal organization. A version of the storage room metaphor occurs in Plato's *Theaetetus*, when Socrates, explaining how one is able to recall particular pieces of information, likens things stored in memory to pigeons housed in a pigeon-coop. This occurrence attests to the antiquity of the idea; indeed, both metaphors, equally visual, equally spatial, seem to be equally ancient as well.

The childhood room, this living heart of memory, situated at the core of *Wielopole, Wielopole* (like the nursery in Anton Chekhov's *Three Sisters*), is a system of backgrounds, a support, or a scene that induces images. Around it, as though summoned, induced by it, is established and radiates all the imagery, the entire thematics of *Wielopole, Wielopole*: the return, the sorrowful experience, age, lost time, and absence. In the course of the performance, the audience witnesses the death of Uncle Józef-Priest; Grandmother Katarzyna carrying out the last rites for him; the three 'dead photographs' of the Priest, the Family, and a group of soldiers – including Kantor's father Marian – before they went to battle; Father Marian and Mother Helka's wedding ceremony; Aunt Mańka's apocalyptic prophecies; the rape of Helka by the soldiers; Adas's mobilization and his departure/funeral in a cattle wagon with a group of conscripts; the funeral of the Priest; the Rabbi's repeated execution by the soldiers; the last gathering of the family interrupted by yet another invasion of the soldiers; and the last group photograph. A constant repetition of the music themes employed in the performance further amplified the theme of memory: Chopin's '*Scherzo*' would emerge every now and then from Uncle Stasio's violin case; a Psalm was sung at the Priest's deathbed; a Polish military march, '*The Grey Infantry*', constantly accompanied the soldiers' presence on stage; and the Rabbi sang an old Yiddish song.

In the end, *Wielopole, Wielopole*, anamnestic activity does not lead to a presence grasped on stage. Kantor, who no longer resides in the childhood house, must resort to the artifice of memory in order to re-animate fantasy and re-activate images, to piece together the simulacrum of a place haunted by absence. This dwelling is not the Edenic microcosm, a welcoming cavity of images. The sort of invention it induces is not as euphoric as it might first seem: abundance is eaten away and neutralized by an irreparable loss.

Remembrance is, in a sense, an inherently dualistic activity. One part of the mind recalls, brings up the past, while the other watches, listens, is reminded, reacts, sometimes refuses the memory brought up, and rejects it. The process of memory retrieval, writes St Augustine,

> brings me out onto the lawns and spacious structures of memory, where treasure is stored, all the representations conveyed there by any of my senses ... Some things, summoned, are instantly delivered up, though others require a longer search, to be drawn from recesses less penetrable.

And all the while, jumbled memories flirt out on their own, interrupting the search for what I want, pestering: Wasn't it us you were seeking? My heart's hand strenuously waves these things away from my memory's gaze, until the dim thing sought arrives at last, fresh from depths. Yet other things are brought up easily, in proper sequence from beginning to end, and laid back in the same order, recallable at will – which happens whenever I recite a literary passage by heart. (Augustin 2002: 49)

The passage offers us a glimpse into the process of gathering memories perfected in medieval monastic meditation, but it also illustrates an instant of mnemotechnical distraction, when the mnemonic pathways leak from one associational network to another. 'The great vice of memoria is not forgetting but disorder', writes Marry Carruthers in *The Craft of Thought*, a study of memory in medieval culture : 'Image "crowding"' or curiositas was considered 'a mnemotechnical vice, because crowding images together blurs them, blocks them, and thus dissipates their effectiveness' (Carruthers 1998: 82). As Carruthers further notes, John Cassian, a medieval mnemonist, categorized this phenomenon as 'a form of mental fornication', 'wandering against having a way or a route' (Carruthers 1998: 83, her emphasis). Although Kantor, like Augustine, can (after 'a longer search') retrieve his buried past, as the performance progresses, it becomes clear that the room of his memory could never be organized. For Augustine, the will ('I') is lord, its ability to 'wave away' and presumably dis-place, with an effort, mnemonic intrusions into an unfrequented corridor of memory is no longer the working assumption. The performance sequences in *Wielopole, Wielopole* were constantly disrupted by the intrusions of phantasmata from behind the doors – the anteroom of history – where 'a storm and inferno rage, / and the waters of the flood rise' (Kantor 1993: 142). Kantor begins by wanting to recollect the past, but memory flooding the stage will prove stronger than his own will. This merging of past and present creates a sense of simultaneity, as in traumatized recall. The insufficiency of voluntary memory – the illusion that the 'storehouse' of images can be locked, unlocked, and used at will – becomes obvious in the scene of rabbi's death.

The scene starts when a rabbi (a character that signifies the Jewish people and its experience during the Second World War) joins a funeral cortege of his deceased friend, a Catholic priest, and starts singing a Jewish popular song: 'Sha Sha Sha de Rebe / Gite / Sha Sha Sha bam reben / Stite / Der shames bad y tur / In di Rebezn oy is duisa / Oy Oy Oy / Oy Oy Oy'.[6] Shot by a group of soldiers, the rabbi collapses to the ground. The dead priest helps him stand up and the rabbi takes up his song again. The soldiers fire from their machine-guns again, and he falls to the ground. This action is repeated a number of times, and then the rabbi leaves.

The death of the rabbi is the central and the most obsessive image of remembering in Kantor's *Wielopole, Wielopole*. This self-reflective exhortation to tell and repeat, to hold on to the past and on to the death by 'calling' it forth through cultural practice, is both a call to active intervention in the discourse of the national remembrance and a mark of Kantor's aesthetics. Every time Kantor replays this violent death on stage, he is doing more than merely returning to a traumatic moment. This procedure – repetitive and obsessive – might be also seen as a way of inducing anxiety, of forcing the spectator to re-experience the (traumatic) explosion of an irreparable past in a way that impedes emotional indifference. These insistent repetitions suggest a hope that, if 'rehearsed' and replayed often enough, the death of the rabbi – this 'memory' so integral to culture and yet only diffusively 'present' within the culture – might also become a collective trauma to be remembered and mourned. What I am trying to emphasize here, calling attention to the way spectators are implicated in the production of images in Kantor's *Wielopole, Wielopole*, is the complex and still contested place of the Holocaust in Polish and European history and culture. Kantor's *Wielopole, Wileopole* and the rest of his memory-theatre could be seen as exercising a certain capacity of moral hospitality to Poland's Jews who died in the war, whose losses in Poland, as in the rest of Europe, were for decades folded into national narratives of mourning and loss, without acknowledging a unique experience of Jewish suffering. Commemorating Polish-Jewish losses as a national trauma, Kantor's theatre could be also seen as a painful yet radical rethinking and reformulation of the very notions of boundaries and borderlines regulating exchange between the inside and the outside, between self and other, indigenous and foreign, offering a vision of Polish identity that incorporates the historical reality of Poland as a set of multicultural communities.

Kantor will be surely remembered as one of the most inventive, articulate, and influential European theatre makers of the twentieth century who sought theatrical forms to communicate the directly experienced or inherited traumas of the Holocaust and other twentieth-century genocides. His theatrical praxis serves as powerful reminder of his unrelenting attempts to invent a new theatrical language of memory in order to release the past from personal and collective oblivion. In that sense it provides an example of a work of mourning in which the ghosts and phantoms of culture are to be entertained rather than exorcized. His performances reframe the question of mourning in ethical terms, functioning as resonant texts, a complicated web of temporality in which memory is not only taken in, introjected, or accrued but reworked, projected, and given back to a collective subject, thus allowing the past to find a 'place' within the identity of the remembering community. Informed by his enormous commitment to witnessing and struggle for justice in the present, they also represent his attempt to do justice to history, make sure that the atrocities of the two world wars could not recur in history, and create the possibility of opening to a different future.

Memory and Theatre in a Global Age

In recent years memory studies has emerged as a truly transnational field of inquiry, moving beyond its early focus on Euro-American events and experiences. Scholars in the field of theatre and performance studies have been at the forefront of this transformation, resituating a study of memory within an international arena and decentring the pattern of Western memory, where unwelcome knowledge, histories, and traumas have been expunged or sanitized. Jean Graham-Jones's *Exorcising History: Argentine Theater under Dictatorship* (2000), Diana Taylor's *The Archive and the Repertoire: Performing Cultural Memory in the Americas* (2003), Ana Elena Puga's *Memory, Allegory, and Testimony in South American Theater: Upstaging Dictatorship* (2008), and Jordana Blejmar's *Playful Memories: The Autofictional Turn in Post-Dictatorship Argentina* (2016), for instance, have explored valences of traumatic memory in the Latin American context, particularly the legacies of centuries of social trauma undergone by many populations in the Americas – from the onset of the colonial conquest to the twentieth-century dictatorships in Uruguay, Chile, Argentina, and other South American countries. Loren Kruger's *Post-Imperial Brecht: Politics and Performance, East and South* (2007), Catherine Cole's *Performing South Africa's Truth Commission: Stages of Transition* (2010), Yvette Hutchison's *South African Performance and the Archives of Memory* (2013), and Mark Fleishman's edited volume *Performing Migrancy and Mobility in Africa: Cape of Flows* (2015) have engaged the difficult legacy of the decades of systematic traumatization of black people by white rulers in South Africa and the social, political, historical, and ethical significance of the Truth and Reconciliation Commission. Emily Roxworthy's *The Spectacle of Japanese American Trauma: Racial Performativity and World War II* (2008) has brought to light the US government's internment policies during the Second World War and their impact on the post-war lives of many Japanese Americans; Diana Looser's *Remaking Pacific Pasts: History, Memory, and Identity in Contemporary Theater from Oceania* (2014) focuses on how Pacific dramatists, actors, and directors have used theatrical performance to critically engage the Pacific's colonial and postcolonial memories and histories; while one of the chapters in *Performance and Cosmopolitics: Cross-Cultural Transactions in Australasia* (2007), co-authored by Helen Gilbert and Jacqueline Lo, examines a variety of artistic and political responses in the Australian context to traumas of the most abject of cosmopolitan subjects – refugees and forced migrants. More so than questions of asylum, in the last two decades the traumas of Australia's 'stolen generations', the survivors and offspring of Indigenous children taken by force from their families in the 1930s through the 1970s and placed in 'white families', have received the attention of theatre and performance scholars (and mainstream representations, including films *Rabbit-Proof Fence* (2002) and *Australia* (2008) directed by Phillip Noyce and Baz Luhrmann respectively, while research on the Truth and Reconciliation Commission of Canada, whose mandate is to learn the truth about what happened in the residential schools across the country, where First Nations, Métis, and Inuit children were placed from the 1870s until 1996, often against their parents' wishes, is already gaining momentum.

Memory and Trauma Studies

Cathy Caruth has suggested that 'trauma itself may provide the very link between cultures' (Caruth 1995: 11), promising cross-cultural listening, and even this cursory look at some recent outputs in the field of theatre and performance studies dealing with historical traumas, violence, and witnessing seems to fulfil this promise. These works show that the interdisciplinary field of theatre and performance studies, involving methodologies from anthropology, history, visual cultures, and critical theory as well as a number of performing arts disciplines such as dance, theatre, and performance art, could be seen as one of the exemplary sites where memory research is productively practised within academic disciplines.

Along with theories of testimony and witnessing, trauma theory has become one of the key modes within which performance and other scholars analyse the transmission of experiences of extreme suffering and violence (and is central to this evolving field of transnational memory studies). However, as Susannah Radstone, one of the leading trauma scholars in the humanities today, argues, 'without careful disciplinary embedding and testing, concepts such as trauma may appear to explain more than they actually can' (Radstone 2008: 35). Furthermore, some of trauma theory's early speculations about processes of memory risk uncritical reception and applications (such as Caruth's formulation of traumatic ordeal) as 'a break in the mind's experience of time' that is characterized by 'the structure of its experience or reception: the event is not assimilated or experienced fully at the time, but only belatedly, in its repeated possession of the one who experiences it' (Caruth 1996: 61; 1995: 4). Radstone also warns that trauma theory 'pays little attention to the question of the fit, or lack of fit between the cultural, local, regional and national knowledges and repertoires of testifier and witness, and neither does it address the differentials of power embedded within any such differences' (Radstone 2011: 117).[3] In a similar vein, in her important book *The Era of the Witness*, the French historian Annete Wieviorka has compellingly argued that to understand how testimony functions in a public sphere, it is necessary to examine the 'circumstances surrounding the act of bearing witness' and the 'larger story' of which it is part (Wieviorka 2006: xiv–xv).

While engaging critically an aspect of trauma theory, which asserts that language or representation fails in the face of trauma, in *Theory for Theatre Studies: Memory*, I argue for the importance of attention to specific articulations of trauma, the range of contexts in which they emerge, and the ways in which cultural differences and regimes of memory in place in particular national settings have affected the manner in which they have been expressed and communicated until today. Ongoing research on the impact of the Holocaust not only on individuals but also on entire communities constitutes one of the most influential strands of research within memory studies. The most influential writings on the traumatic legacies of the Holocaust and challenges it poses for witnessing emerged in the 1980s in the United States. For instance, certain core assumptions informing these conceptions of trauma have not gone uncontested. In her book *Holocaust and Memory (Zagłada i pamiec')*, the Polish sociologist Barbara Engelking explores, among other subjects, the psychological consequences of wartime experiences for Jewish Holocaust survivors still living in Poland, questioning what she sees as hardening orthodoxies of memory studies. Engelking writes:

> It would seem that the [Anglo-Saxon] researchers take a position similar to that of wartime witnesses to the Holocaust: in discerning only the medical, pathological consequences of these experiences, they place the experiences themselves beyond the bounds of the understandable, interpretable world. They close them up in a great cupboard with a notice reading 'Dysfunction' or 'Psychopathology,' which provides an alibi for not taking part in other people's suffering... Researches into wartime experiences therefore join, willy nilly, the 'conspiracy of silence' [that]... really began with absence of reaction on the part of the world to the Holocaust during the war, and it goes on until today. (Engelking 2001: 267)

According to Engelking, knowledge about traumatic experiences and their consequences, 'which was built up mainly on the basis of American research, took insufficient notice of cultural differences between pre- and postwar communities of survivors, and the influence of these differences on their psychological well-being' (Engelking 2001: 267). The survivors who found themselves in the United States after the war could not communicate their traumas to the society that had not shared their wartime experiences.

> And apart from wartime experiences, their baggage contained value systems shaped in the pre-war world. This could mean that the survivors themselves had difficulty in adapting to the new universal cultural and moral values that were so different from the ones they had lost. From this point of view, some of their problems could be seen as a research artefact which resulted to a great extent not from the very essence of the experience of war, but from a confrontation between these experiences and the postwar world which did not understand them and was not understood by them, and had a different civilisational and cultural existence. (Engelking 2001: 268)

Engelking also alludes to the difficulties survivors experienced in rendering their experiences in foreign languages, which they had learnt only after the war. So while the stand of trauma theory that dominates the humanities today was largely informed by the experiences of the Holocaust survivors who found themselves in the United States after the war, Engelking believes that 'accounts by Polish survivors in Polish are more reliable, closer to the inner truth, than accounts given in other languages' (Engelking 2001: 269).

While Engelking emphasizes how important it is to pay attention to aspects of the location in which memories are transmitted, in an essay on Soviet memories, Catherine Merridale questions the universalization of trauma theory and its applicability to the traumatic legacies of the Soviet era. After conducting an oral history project with Gulag survivors and Red Army veterans from the Second World War in Russia in the 1990s, this historian concluded that the classic story of trauma's legacy, the medical diagnosis of posttraumatic stress disorder (PTSD) now so universally accepted, simply misses the point in the Soviet case. It is irrelevant because it is an import to the Soviet situation, a discovery that suggests that, while suffering is universal, the reactions to it, especially at the social level, are culturally specific. (Merridale 2010: 379–80)

Merridale's contention that there is a misfit between globalizing trauma theory and localized social realities related to the Soviet case as well as her implicit claim that trauma homogenizes all victims and obliterates experience are true to a point but also could be more nuanced. While her stance is not universally shared among scholars writing on the cultural memory of the Soviet terror (see, for instance, Cherkaev 2014; Etkind 2013), it gestures to a crucial linkage between the individual and the social in the context of human suffering. The devastating experiences of the Second World War and the Gulags that gave rise to trauma, pain, and other disorders could be seen as principally psychological or medical, and hence, individual; yet, they are also social, political, and cultural matters. Something gets lost, argues Merridale, when the local idioms of victims are translated into the universal language of trauma, thereby remaking the experiences of suffering.

Merridale's reservations about the usefulness of existing conceptions of trauma for analysing the traumatic disruptions peculiar to twentieth-century Soviet history spring also from other concerns, which she shares with some postcolonial scholars (for instance, Glissant 1989; Khanna 2003). For one, trauma theory's insistence on the individual psyche fails to account not only for the collective nature of the trauma in the Soviet case but also its long duress. As some critics note – especially those who consider 'postcolonial' trauma's place in contemporary trauma theory – 'there is a need to expand our understanding of trauma from sudden, unexpected catastrophic events' in order 'to encompass ongoing, everyday forms of violence and oppression affecting subordinate groups' (Craps

2010: 54). They advocate a model of trauma that would reflect the experience of subaltern groups by bringing to light their 'chronic psychic suffering' endured through '[e]xposure to acts or threats of physical and psychological violence' (Craps 2010: 55).[4] Rather than being a break from the norm, an interruption of the existing sense of the self as anchored in a decipherable past, then, trauma can be endured over a long period of time. Édouard Glissant's analogy between the individual psyche and the collective neurosis that sheds light on the relation between structural and historical traumas brought on by slavery; the destruction of aboriginal communities; and genocide, imperialistic, and postimperialistic oppression in the Antilles is apt here. He asks:

> Would it be ridiculous to consider our lived history as a steadily advancing neurosis? To see the Slave Trade as a traumatic shock, our relocation (in the new land) as a repressive phase, slavery as the period of latency, 'emancipation' in 1848 as reactivation, our everyday fantasies as symptoms, and even our horror of 'returning to those things of the past' as possible manifestation of the neurotic's fear of his past? (Glissant 1989: 65–6)

Furthermore, the workings of inter- and transgenerational transmission of trauma bring to the fore a related yet distinct set of issues for the children of survivors and those of their generation born in the aftermath of histories of violence such as war, slavery, and expulsion, who connect so deeply to the past they have never directly experienced that they insist on the term 'memory' to describe that connection. Marianne Hirsch, a US-based literary critic, has named this phenomenon 'postmemory': 'identification with the victim or witness of trauma, modulated by an admission of an unbridgeable distance separating the participant from the one born after' (Hirsch 1999: 8). Postmemory also entails reaching across lines of difference to the experience of others to whom one is not related by blood, a kind of connective memory work that could engender 'transnational interconnections and intersections in a global space of remembrance' (Hirsch 2012: 247).

The performances of memory among Eastern European Jews and their descendants who still feel and seek a connection to their roots through the layered and fragmented memory left to them represent one such postmemorial landscape. Since the fall of the Berlin Wall, and the transformation of the Eastern bloc, many such individuals have travelled to their ancestral sites in Eastern Europe, which – as their travelogues confirm – still constitute an integral part of their identity. *Ghosts of Home: The Afterlife of Czernowitz in Jewish Memory* (2010), written collaboratively by Hirsch and the historian Leo Spitzer, is an excellent example here. It offers a rich account of Czernowitz, a multicultural, tolerant place in the former Austro-Hungarian Empire, whose heir, the city of Chernivtsi, emerged after the Second World War and the Holocaust as an almost homogeneous Ukrainian city. Hirsch and Spitzer's project involved heritage trips to this city in the south-western part of Ukraine, together with Hirsch's parents, Holocaust survivors who came from Czernowitz. Drawing on personal interviews, published memoirs by German-Jewish Czernowitzers, and their own second-generation experiences and inherited memories, Hirsch and Spitzer draw a fascinating portrait of Czernowitz, accounting for its many ethnic and cultural transformations: from the Habsburg era, when German-Jewish culture flourished in the city, to the contemporary period. Hirsh explains her reasons for going to Chernivtsi early on in the book. 'I grew up in 1950s Bucharest, Romania, within a community of fellow Germanspeaking exiles from Czernowitz whose tastes, attitudes, behaviours, and stories about a world that had long ceased to exist shaped me profoundly', she writes. 'My desire to visit Czernowitz originated with these encounters and grew in intensity over many years' (Hirsch and Spitzer 2010: 9). After she and her parents moved to Austria in 1961 and then to the United States in 1962, for Hirsch her 'parents' city of origin acquired an even more distant, mythic aura' (Hirsch and Spitzer 2009: 10).

In her recent work, Jordana Blejmar (2017) has discussed the theatricalization of this memory discourse by addressing the links between memory, politics, and performance in the works of the so-called 'postmemory generations' in Latin America, comprised of those who were born or grew up during the dictatorships and internal conflicts that shattered the region during the second half of the twentieth century. The exponents of this kind of theatre practice, she argues, claim that (post)memory is not merely a 'familial' and private issue but a collective effort and that more expansive and queered communities of what Marianne Hirsch has called an 'affiliative postmemory' (2012) are necessary to reconstruct the fibres of political and social life in Latin America. Moreover, (post)memory is conceived here not so much as a representation or a re-enactment of the past but as a political intervention in the present.

Memory and Mourning and Melancholia

Throughout *Theory for Theatre Studies: Memory*, I also address loss, something that has come to interest many theatre practitioners and scholars, political theorists, museum curators, feminists, psychoanalysts, and AIDS activists, who grapple with the humane and productive possibilities in the workings of witness, memory, and melancholy. If trauma 'always makes itself felt viscerally in the here and now' (Taylor 2006: 1675), such traumatic fusing of past and present is also characteristic of melancholy. As Kathleen Biddick argues, drawing on Freud: 'To unfuse past, present, and future, to return to the narrative relation of temporality, requires the work of mourning. Mourning does not find the lost object; it acknowledges its loss, thus allowing the lost object to be lost while maintaining a narrative connection to it' (Biddick 2007: 10).

Freud's writings on mourning and melancholia consist primarily of the well-known essay entitled 'Mourning and Melancholia' (1917 [1957]), and 'On Transience' (1915). In 'Mourning and Melancholia', which has defined the study of loss for much of the last century, he seeks to explain the distinction between a normal and pathological affect occasioned by the death of an object of love (be it a beloved person or an abstract ideal). For Freud, mourning is the attenuated detachment of the libido from the object that had been charged or cathected by the ego. Although mourning is invariably difficult in that 'libido clings to its objects and will not [willingly] renounce those that are lost even when a substitute lies ready to hand' (Freud [1915] 1957: 306–7), the resolution of grief is nonetheless complete when the ego succeeds in detaching itself from the past through either the replacement of a cherished object with a new one or the temporary return of libido to the ego. Thus, Freud argues, a successful work of mourning constitutes an articulated reaction to loss: the loss is recognized by the subject and separated from the body through the recognition of what has been lost. What is 'recognized' is both separated from the body and simultaneously interiorized within the body through a kind of psychic assimilation.

In contrast to mourning, melancholia is characterized by the inability of the subject to separate itself from the object (i.e. by the ego's identification with the lost object) and an essential misrecognition of what has been lost. As Freud puts it, 'melancholia is in some way related to an object-loss which is withdrawn from consciousness, in contradistinction to mourning, in which there is nothing about the loss that is unconscious' (Freud [1917] 1957: 245). In other words, the difference between a 'normal' and 'pathological' affect here is that in mourning the lost object is always perceived as distinct and existing outside of the ego, while in melancholia that what has been lost constitutes an enigma. And while in both mourning and melancholia, the subject dwells on the past, the melancholic appears unable to leave the past behind – grief does not end.

Ultimately, Freud's initial confidence in the possibility of successful mourning without residue appears to waver. Although in 'Mourning and Melancholia' he posits the resolution of grief through the withdrawal of libidinal energy from an object, in 'The Ego and the Id' (1955 [1923]), he comes to view mourning and melancholia as processes that instead deepen the relation to the object, allowing the very formation of identification (Freud 1955 [1923]: 28–9). In other words, while in the initial essay, Freud regards identification as being exclusively the preserve of the melancholic ego, he later comes to regard it as a necessary component of the functioning of the psyche.

In *The Psychic Life of Power*, Judith Butler expands upon Freud's findings from *The Ego and the Id*, where he comes to see the ego as a precipitate of lost attachments, as well as upon Nicolas Abraham's and Maria Torok's insights into the structures of incorporative melancholia (on which I will expand below). Butler argues that melancholia is 'precisely what interiorises the psyche, that is, makes it possible to refer to the psyche through such topographical tropes. The turn from object to ego is the movement that makes the distinction between them possible, that marks the division, the separation or loss, that forms the ego to begin with' (Butler 1997a: 170). Like Butler, Julia Kristeva describes melancholia as a condition for the constitution of the subject.

In *Black Sun: Depression and Melancholia* (1989), Kristeva reiterates and reworks the classic psychoanalytic conception of melancholy (Abraham, Freud, Melanie Klein) that detects in it intolerance for object loss; she comes to present melancholy as a formative loss that is prior to object love, ultimately associated with the maternal body. The special focus of *Black Sun* is what befalls the primitive self in respect to the archaic and incomplete parting from the mother: the shadow cast on the fragile self by the impact of primal loss. The depressed person is not the prisoner and guardian of a lost object but the prisoner and guardian of an affect recording immemorial loss. Thus, both Kristeva and Butler extend classic psychoanalytic theory of melancholy in the same direction when they suggest that melancholia is an essential prerequisite for the subject and object formation. In his writings, Freud often presented introjection and incorporation, two crucial analytical concepts for an exploration of the concepts of mourning and melancholia, as synonymous. Nicolas Abraham and Maria Torok (1994) have enriched our understanding of these phenomena through their insistence on the distinction between introjection (successful mourning) and incorporation (pathological forms and variations of mourning) and by proposing the notion of a 'psychic crypt'. Such a space, they suggest, is often generated by the trauma of object-loss and an impossible mourning it effects; the lost object is kept inside the self unconsciously, as though buried alive. And while in mourning, psychic pain can gain access to symbolization, in melancholia, there is an inability to symbolize due to the encryptment of the death of the other. Abraham and Torok further explain this phenomenon by introducing a concept of a 'supplemental topography' (Abraham and Torok 1994: 135) entombed in the psyche so that the need to acknowledge the loss of a love object and the need to mourn it need never be avowed. In an effort to preserve itself from the demands of reality that threatens to cause the change, the subject stands divided against itself, while the distinctions between inside and outside, subject and object, active and passive become blurred. As Abraham and Torok write:

> To state that endocryptic identification is the work of fantasy alone means that its content amounts to maintaining the illusion of the topographical status quo, as it had not been prior to the covert transformation. As for the inclusion itself, it is not fantasy. Inclusion attests to a painful reality, forever denied: the 'gaping wound' of topography. (Abraham and Torok 1994: 142)

The authors further explain that against the gradual and possibly long-drawn libidinal re-investment which the recognition and acceptance of what has been lost entail, 'the magical "cure" by incorporation exempts the subject from the painful process of reorganisation. When in the form of imaginary or real nourishment, we ingest the love-object we miss, this means that we refuse to mourn and thus we shun the consequences of mourning even though our psyche is fully bereaved' (Abraham and Torok 1994: 127).[5]

The sections that follow build on core debates in several of these and other texts by paying attention to the historical as well as gendered dimension of performance's power to witness the acts of violence that often go missing in public discourses and culture. They will further demonstrate the status of memory as a contested form of social, cultural, and political practice central to current academic debates on memory across disciplines, including theatre studies. Focusing in particular on themes of reconciliation, reparation, and migrations, they will show that the interdisciplinary field of theatre and performance studies, involving as it does methodologies from anthropology, history, visual cultures, critical theory, as well as a number of performing arts disciplines such as theatre, performance art, and dance, should be seen as one of the exemplary sites where memory research is productively practised within the academy.

SECTION TWO

Searching for a Common Ground: Performance, Testimony, and Small Acts of Repair

In one of the central scenes of Katie Mitchell's *The Forbidden Zone* (2014), Fritz Haber – the German scientist principally responsible for the development of poison gas in the First World War – narrates how, as the spring day of 22 April 1915 drew to a close, German soldiers released cylinders of chlorine gas against the Allies entrenched around Langemarck, near Ypres. What happened next was one of the most frightening and horrific experiences ever faced by men at war. As the acrid cloud enveloped the soldiers, they began to cough, clutch their throats, and gasp for air. Many turned blue and fell to the ground dead. Those who were able to escape stumbled into first-aid stations where doctors were unable to provide any effective medical treatment. Haber closes his testimony by describing how the German soldiers tried to save the lives of their French counterparts in the enemy's trenches by giving them their own breathing equipment.

The conditions were perfect. The wind was moving directly towards the French lines. There was excellent visibility. From my vantage point I had a clear view of the field. Things proceeded as per my calculations. We released the cylinders. Nearly six thousand of them over six and a half kilometers.

The sheet of gas swamped the field. Through my binoculars I could see nothing but white.

It reached the first French line. The guns stopped firing.

I could hear distant birdsong. The stream. Wind. It was as if there was no war.

I advised that our troops should advance towards the French lines. They weren't prepared for the absolute success of the attack. Many of our men fell. Many remained for too long in the enemy dug-out.

They were helping the French soldiers. Giving them their own breathing equipment. Advantage was not taken. In no future war will the military be able to ignore poison gas. It is a higher form of killing. (*Macmilan*, unpublished ms)

This unexpected act of solidarity witnessed by Haber, which for a moment transformed the 'ghostly frontline', to use Benjamin's term, into a common ground affirming their shared humanity, serves as a point of departure for this chapter, in which I will discuss theatre as a common ground for empathetic experiences as well as a site where those who care about justice can also confront their own assumptions about autonomy, liberty, and responsibility.

The case studies that this chapter explores are Lola Arias's *Minefield/Campo minado* (UK/Argentina) from 2016, Yael Ronen's *Common Ground* (Germany/Bosnia and Herzegovina) from 2014, and Robert Lepage's *The Seven Streams of the River Ota* (Canada) from 1994 to 1998. Through the interplay between repetition and immediacy, and between theatricality and performativity, these performances formulate an exemplary repertoire of strategies for exploring memories of war, conflict, and recently contested pasts.

Ronen's *Common Ground*, which premiered at the Maxim Gorki Theatre in Berlin, portrays a group of people from the former Yugoslavia who were forced to migrate after the wars of the 1990s, coming from Belgrade, Sarajevo, Novi Sad, and Prijedor to Berlin. What is their common ground? The theatre company developed the play collectively based on its trip to Bosnia and meetings with both experts on Yugoslav Wars and family members of the actors, whose lives were put on stage. As stated on the theatre's website, the play's intention is to provide 'a safe space for discussing terms like guilt and atonement, forgiveness and forgetting, while stereotypes, prejudices and conflicting narratives gleefully collide' (Ronen 2014).

Minefield was first staged in May and June 2016 at the Brighton Theatre Festival and at London's Royal Court Theatre as part of the LIFT festival, respectively. With a combination of film, acting, and testimonies, as well as technology, and thunderous rock and punk music, Arias puts on stage three former Argentine soldiers along with three British counterparts. Among the Argentines are: Marcelo Vallejo, formerly a member of a mortar team and now a champion triathlete; Rubén Otero, a survivor of the sinking of the ARA *General Belgrano* and now a member of a Beatles tribute band, the Get Back Trio; and Gabriel Sagastume, previously a soldier and now a criminal attorney. On the British side are: Lou Armour, a former prisoner of the Argentinian forces and now a special-needs teacher; David Jackson, who during the war worked in intelligence and is now a psychologist; and Sukrim Rai, a Nepalese Ghurka who fought in the war and only recently acquired British citizenship. The six performers narrate and re-enact different aspects of the Falklands war in chronological order, over the show's course addressing the reasons that led them to join the army, whether they killed someone or witnessed the deaths of their fellow soldiers, how they were received when they returned home, and what they do now, more than thirty years after the war.

The play explores topics that have defined most of Arias' oeuvre, with theatre serving as a medium to revive the past and recover lost, or blocked, memories, fuelled by the idea of performance as a dynamic exchange between life and stage, with concrete effects on the lives of audiences and performers. I am particularly interested in a closer look at Arias' conception of theatre as a 'living creature' and a highly unpredictable 'social experiment', which is how she described this performance in a lecture that she gave on 6 June 2016, at King's College, London. Her experimental gathering of performers from the two sides of the war on memory's tricky terrain presents a series of challenges, including the risk of re-traumatization through the recollection of painful wartime and post-war experiences. I will argue, however, that Arias not only successfully overcomes these risks but also demonstrates theatre's capacity to serve as a shared ground for empathetic encounters between former enemies, for recognition of their mutual grievances and abuses perpetrated by the military, and for mourning of their losses.

The twentieth century (and I limit myself to that period in this chapter) was an era perhaps unparalleled in the number and variety of extreme and horrendous events and experiences to which people were subjected in many parts of the world: the massacre of the Armenians between 1914 and 1918; the rape of Nanking; the firestorms in Hamburg and Dresden during the allied bombing raids of the Second World War; the concentration and extermination camps; Hiroshima and Nagasaki; Vietnam; Cambodia; brutal dictatorships in Central and South America and elsewhere (notably Africa); and all the genocides and ethnocides of indigenous peoples in many parts of the globe. To try to list them all is a self-defeating task. Furthermore, each of them has its historical specificity, which determines the characteristics of the witnessing associated with it in key ways. In other words, not only the historical experiences themselves but also the accounts of given historical experiences are significantly different.

Yet the witnessing of atrocity, as I will show here in my analysis of Robert Lepage's *The Seven Streams of the River Ota*, my third case study here, is also a practice that presents significant regularities, independently of the vast range of circumstances in which people live through traumatic events. As Ross Chambers argues, 'there is always an experience that the sufferer judges atrocious and is in a position to bear witness to; there is likewise the act of witness itself ..., and finally ... the conditions of its reception' (2004: 6). It is out of the relations between these constants that the possibility of generalizing about witnessing as a practice emerges, even while we remain attentive to different social arenas in which struggles over the past play out. *The Seven Streams of the River Ota* was originally created to commemorate the fiftieth anniversary of the Hiroshima bombing, while also remembering the Holocaust and the AIDS crisis of the 1980s and 1990s in the West. Asking how and why these histories are imagined in relation to each other, I address the ethical and political problems that attend to the circulation of memories. Finally, I show how postgenerations haunted by stories that have not been worked through still find that they owe the victims acts of attentive listening and historical repair.

Theatre and Small Acts of Repair

Reparations have a long history dating back at least to the first Punic War in the third century BCE, when Rome imposed monetary payments on a defeated Carthage. Today, reparations signal the convergence of a number of political and social justice movements seeking redress for state-sponsored and extra-state violence, injury, and harm. In its most common usage, writes Marianne Hirsch, reparation is an ethico-political and legal concept – a public acknowledgement of injury by a state or state-connected institution, and a compensatory settlement that often, but not always, involves a monetary award (2017: 17). The concept of reparation is central also in psychoanalysis, however, yet its political and psychic genealogies are rarely discussed in relation to one another. As a key concept in psychoanalysis, and specifically in object relations theory, reparation signifies the repairing of harm on the psychic rather than social level. In Melanie Klein's key account of child development, reparation is delineated as an intrapsychic process that enables an infant (and, by extension, an adult) to attain healthy intellectual and psychological development and a secure grasp of reality. Through this process, the infant learns to manage its ambivalent relationship to the mother – for instance, due to indignant rage, or phantasies of aggression and injury – so that 'love [can be] freed' (Klein 1986: 163). In 'Love, Guilt, and Reparation', Klein tells us that 'making reparation … is a fundamental element in love and in all human relationships' (1937: 313). She relates the urge to repair to a prior 'capacity to identify ourselves with the loved person' that we have injured in unconscious phantasy (1937: 311). As David Eng notes in his reading of Klein, this is a powerful account of the 'emergence of morality' (2016: 14). The focus on the preservation of love in Klein's psychic account of reparation might thus be seen as an attempt to shift the inexorable negativity of the death drive, and its will to destruction, in a more productive and moral direction. For reparation to take place, however, the infant must first decide that an object is worth saving. Since Klein explicitly makes identification with loved others the pivot for the reparative turn, she narrows the circle of those whose injuries we feel pulled to redress. Indeed, as Eng argues, such conceptualization may even limit our capacity to recognize some injuries as injuries at all (2016: 8).

Eng unpacks political consequences of this insight in his article 'Colonial Object Relations':

> For reparation to occur, there must be an awareness of loss, a feeling of guilt, an apprehension of dependency, but what of the loss of an object that does not result in such

acknowledgements? In this regard, reparation in Klein might be said to institute a dividing line between the good and the bad itself – indeed, retroactively constituting a field of good and bad objects precisely through the management of love and the regulation of hate ordered by a long history of colonial morality and liberal reason. (2016: 9)

I will come back to this important issue later, when addressing the psychic complexities of the work of reparation in relation to the three mentioned performances. At this point, a closer look at the ways in which psychic genealogies of reparation supplement and interrupt both political and ethical possibilities of reparation and reconciliation is needed.

In her introduction to a special issue of the journal *Memory Studies*, titled 'Reconciliation and Memory: Critical Perspectives', Ann Rigney argues that the traumatic paradigm that came to dominate conceptualizations of memory and its practices in the decades following the Second World War is now morphing into something new under the influence of a global discourse of human rights and the legal practices associated with it, including legal tribunals, truth commissions, official apologies, and reparations (2012: 252). For Rigney, reconciliation practices such as the South African Truth and Reconciliation Commission (TRC) occur in 'a liminal period marking the passage from old to new and providing a delimited space of negotiation' (2012: 252). She argues that reconciliation practices, albeit fraught with moral, emotive, and political difficulties, nevertheless constitute a bridge between a present held captive by a traumatic past and the 'slow' time of reconciliation. In the time of reconciliation, the discourse and practice of reparative remembrance can render the past as past and take leave of painful legacies, leaving the way open to a possibly different future. On this account, traumatic and reparative remembering are differentiated not just by their temporalities but also by witnessing relations to testimony that they engage. As Susannah Radstone puts it, 'If the witnessing process associated with trauma aims to translate unremembered wounds into narrative memory's present, leaving the way open for their eventual consignment to the past, reparative remembering constitutes the next step, transforming the "presentness" of these memories into a publicly acknowledged and pragmatically agreed "past"' (2017: 652–3).

How can violent histories find redress through theatre? As discussed in this book's introduction, a number of theatre and performance studies scholars and practitioners have grappled with this question in the aftermath of violent histories in places such as Argentina and Chile (Taylor 2003; Blejmar 2017/18), Columbia (Estrada Fuentes 2017), South Africa (Cole 2010; Hutchinson 2013; Fleishman 2015), the Balkans, Israel/Palestine (Kuftinec 2009), and Oceania (Looser 2014), to name just some of the relevant geographies and scholars. Sonja Kuftinec's book, for instance, offers valuable insights into the ethics of facilitation and the question of how theatre may contribute to the transformation of a conflict situation and the rebuilding of a community in areas of violent group contestation in Bosnia and Herzegovina, Croatia, Macedonia, Bulgaria, Israel, and the occupied Palestinian territories. Drawing on her experience with many community-based projects in which she participated since 1995 as a facilitator, director, or witness, she asserts that theatre is particularly suited to providing a dialectical modality for conflict resolution in conflict-ridden contexts due to its ability to illuminate collisions of simultaneous truths, rather than insistence on the binary presentation of conflicts. Asserting that ideological conflicts can be bridged by shifting attention from nation formation to ethical communities, Kuftinec considers theatrical facilitations that denaturalize ethnic and national identities, invite active witnessing, and allow participants to animate collective memories that tell an alternative history. While often grappling with how to negotiate between articulating hope and witnessing pain and suffering, she conceives of theatre as a performative utopia that 'offers a site for face-to-face nonviolent encounters with the Other, prompting a development of ethical relationships' (2009: 110). While these encounters may not immediately convene other future life-worlds, or completely rewrite the individual's narrative of social or national belonging, she believes that they provide the groundwork for future improvement in both regards: 'Imagining those different futures through a kind of activist empathy forges temporary ethical communities in relation with rather than in opposition to another' (2009: 25). Ultimately, she believes that 'The forging of ethical communities on this micro plane may lead to more far-reaching social transformation at the macro level of the nation' (2009: 25). As my analysis of *Minefield*, *Common Ground*, and *The Seven Streams of the River Ota* will show, Arias, Ronen, and Lepage work in a similar vein to create spaces where our connection to past and present injustices can be enacted, critiqued, and remembered by all participants. Their works show that this is a continuous process, with all of its participants repeatedly confronting their own implication in difficult histories and demonstrate that 'theatrical facilitations are vital not because of the answers provided, but because the questions enabled can enact our very being through the presence of others' (Kuftinec 2009: 80).

Case Study 1: Lola Arias' *Minefield*

As she explained in a recent interview, work on *Minefield* started with a single question she asked her cast: 'What is the memory [connected to the war experience] that stayed in your mind until today?' (qtd. in Bither 2019: n.p.). She did not want them to tell her their whole war story, but only of the memory that remained engraved in their mind and returned to them in flashbacks, the image that followed them like a ghost. In prompting her actors to try to find this image, this one strong memory, rather than relying on often retold anecdotes, Arias is akin to the generation of artists that the Dutch historian Ernst Van Alphen had praised for their 'purposeful attempts to shed the mastery that Holocaust narratives provide', which 'entice the viewer to enter into a relationship that is affective and emotional rather than cognitive' (2005: 201). In Arias' words, 'going back to this deep memory was a big part of the process of trying to find out what is the most painful thing that comes back, and then we tried to build up their stories from there' (qtd. in Bither 2019: n.p.).

The director recalls how Marcelo [Vallejo] wrote in his diary once:

> I am in a rehearsal. I hear the voices of the British people saying, 'Give back your weapons.' Weapons and helmets, weapons and helmets. And I realized the sound of this voice brings me back to the end of the war, and I'm going back to what I felt when I had to give back my helmet and my weapon, and I felt lonely and lost and [asking] what did I fight for? (qtd. in Bither 2019: n.p.)

As this example shows, the fact that the performers heard voices of their former enemies during the rehearsal process, speaking a language that most of them did not even understand at the time of recalled events, exhumed real memories that remained hidden until then.

While acknowledging the painstaking process of digging into memory as deeply as possible to go beyond the anecdote and find its missing parts, Arias also accounts for the contractedness of memory that inevitably manifests in such endeavours. As she states, 'at some point you have to know that we are all writing the novels of our lives, and we are all making up things and adding details that never happened. And we don't even know at some point in our lives which are the details that we added over years or what really happened' (qtd. in Bither 2019: n.p.). This insight especially holds true for traumatic memories. As Cathy Caruth has noted, 'the transformation of the trauma into a narrative memory that allows the story to be verbalised and communicated, to be integrated into one's own, and others', knowledge of the past, may lose both the precision and the force that characterizes traumatic recall' (1995: 153). When relating the story of Pierre Janet's patient Irène, for instance, Caruth explains that 'her cure is characterised by the fact that she can tell a "slightly different story" to different people' (1995: 153). In other words, the capacity to remember is linked also to the capacity to shape the narrative, or even to forget it.

Arias' reflections on the subjective nature of memory resonate with the epigram to 'None of Us Will Return' ('Aucun de nous ne reviendra'), the first part of Charlotte Delbo's memoir *Auschwitz and After* (*Auschwitz et après* 1995): 'Today, I am not sure that what I wrote is true. I am certain it is truthful' (qtd. in Hirsch and Spitzer 2009: 160). To Marianne Hirsch and Leo Spitzer, 'Delbo could be saying that today, in the space of the "after" (*Auschwitz and After*), she no longer recalls the exact facts, but that she is certain she is conveying a deeper truth about her camp experience, its essence, its deep memory' (2009: 160). If deep memory defies historicization and resists turning into a controlled narrative, threatening to collapse the distinction between past and present and to re-engulf the survivor, what can theatre do to responsibly address historical trauma on stage? Tavia Nyong'o looks at this question in his contribution to *Thinking through Theatre and Performance*, where he considers how theatre might consciously extend its responsibility towards historically and socially important – but potentially traumatic – material, which might, intentionally or otherwise, 'trigger' both performers and spectators. Discussing 'trigger warnings' and art's obligations – or otherwise – to the sensibilities of its participants and consumers, he argues that contemporary theatre does not offer a straightforward, universal answer to the question of the ethics of representing historical trauma. Rather, drawing on psychoanalytic theory, specifically the object-relations school associated with Melanie Klein, Donald Winnicott, and others, he argues that 'at its best, theatre creates a *good enough holding environment* ... in which trauma can be encountered, as it were, non-traumatically' (Nyong'o 2019: 203). On this account, 'the apparent impossibility of such a "trigger free" theatre should not dissuade theatre artist from rigorously searching for an ethics of rehearsal, performance and after-care, based on the absence of trauma or re-traumatizing, but upon an alert and dynamic response to triggering when and where it occurs' (2019: 200).

So, how might performance meet and tame trauma on the terrain of repetition? As Richard Schechner famously posited, 'Performance means: never for the first time. It means: for the second to the nth time. Performance is "twice-behaved behavior"' (1985: 36). The same could be said of trauma. As Diana Taylor states, 'Like performance, trauma always makes itself felt viscerally in the here and now. Past blows haunt our present and shake the individual and social body' (2006: 1675). Crucially, trauma is also never for the first time – at least until the traumatic event is given meaning and integrated into the survivor's consciousness. This being said, it is important to remember something that Rebecca Schneider underlines, namely that what returns, or what 'appears in the syncopated time of citational performance', is not 'presence', but 'precisely (again) the missed encounter – the reverberations of the overlooked, the missed, the repressed, the seemingly forgotten' (2011: 102).

As my first example from *Minefield* suggests, an epistemic mastery of what happened always remains in tension with a performative mastery of emotions triggered by the given event. In the scene that lends the play its title, *Minefield*, all six performers reconstruct an episode in which Argentinian soldiers stationed on Mount Longdon, famished after days without supplies, went out in search of food. They found food in a house nearby, though across a river, along with a small wooden boat in which they could transport the supplies. On their way back, however, as they walk with the upturned boat held above their heads (for they wish to keep it for the future), they stumble onto a minefield and all of them are killed. Gabriel tells the story to the audience using plastic toy soldiers and a miniature model landscape, which are projected onto a big screen shaped like an open book standing on end. He explains that he witnessed the scene of carnage because he and a superior officer were asked to gather the soldiers' remains in a blanket and take them back to the base. In the process, he recognizes a football sock on one of the dismembered body parts as belonging to his friend.

To be sure, Arias' method of using re-enactment to recall historical events in this work is not exclusive to art. Re-enactments exist across a range of popular activities, with the term 're-enactment' covering a wide range of forms and practices, as Rebecca Schneider points out in *Performing Remains*: from re-playing or re-doing a precedent event, artwork, or act to historical re-enactments in living history museums, historical reality television shows, and preservation societies. What all of these forms and practices have in common is the central value they assign to memory. 'In many ways', writes Schneider, 'reenactment has become the popular and practice-based wing of what has been called the twentieth-century academic "memory industry"' (2011: 2). Indeed, the significance of memory to the use of re-enactments in contemporary art and performance is hard to miss. While harnessed to a variety of aesthetic and political goals and using different means to engage their audiences, such re-enactments all share 'an interest in how time, memory, and history work – and how or whether we can retrieve past events … by redoing them in some fashion' (Jones 2011: 24–5).

To Vanessa Agnew, contemporary re-enactment is indicative of the recent 'affective turn' in the study of history and marks a departure from more traditional forms of historiographical inquiry. From her perspective, '[as] a form of affective history – i.e. historical representation that both takes affect as its object and attempts to elicit affect – reenactment is less concerned with events, processes, or structures than with the individual's physical and psychological experience' (2007: 301). Schneider makes a similar observation in accounting for the continued popular appeal of Civil War re-enactments in the United States, noting: 'The *feel* – the affective engagement – is key' (2011: 50). She concluded from her interviews and observations of re-enactors that they 'wanted to touch something they deemed authentic, real, and actual in experience – something about fighting and falling on the field that would be other than what they could glean from textual accounts, photographic images, or watching film actors reenacting on screen' (2011: 54). In other words, these people 'wanted to *experience it for themselves* and add to their historical acumen by way of their own physical engagement' (2011: 54; original emphasis). In the *Minefield* scene, however, something else appears to be at stake.

In this scene, and indeed in the rest of *Minefield*, history was 'presented as a "story", since it was explicitly partial, subjective, affective and imaginative, rather than claiming to constitute a sequence of "facts"' (Finburgh 2017: 174). Moreover, Arias employs distancing devices throughout the performance, such as toys, DIY construction of narrative, and the 'the techniques and devices that serve to create the kind of high-definition realism that habitually represents our world via the dominant televisual media' (Finburgh 2017: 174). In so doing, she lays bare the necessary constructedness of all historical narratives while also providing a 'holding' (if never entirely safe) environment for her performers to reckon with their past.

It is only later in life that Gabriel learns that the field was mined by the Argentine armed forces rather than the enemy. By communicating this fact at the end of this emotional scene, Arias underlines for the audience the story of a failure, including 'the flawed logistics and poor strategic leadership the men suffered' (Delgado 2019: n.p.). In a recent interview, she highlighted how this was an integral part of her dramaturgical vision and how she struggled with her actors sometimes because they wanted, or needed (perhaps in more unconscious ways), to be portrayed as heroes. In this, Arias is like one of her influences, Svetlana Alexievich, the 2015 Nobel Prize winner in Literature from Belarus who offers non-redemptive and non-heroic accounts of the events of the Great Patriotic War in books such as *War's Unwomanly*

Face (2012 [1985]) and *Last Witnesses* (2004 [1985]). Like Alexievich, Arias is a woman writing the stories of men to reveal another aspect of a historical event, the missing parts of the whole narrative.

'In the Introduction, I have referred to Butler's remark that 'no one has ever worked through an injury without repeating it' (1997b: 102), thus raising the question about the purpose of restaging traumatic events and reviving the attached affects. This concern is certainly relevant for the second scene from *Minefield* I want to look at here. In it, Lou (Armour) narrates how he shot an Argentine soldier in the face just before realizing that he had probably wanted to surrender and how he then died in his arms. His first account of this event came in an interview for a documentary programme made in England only months after the war – Peter Kosminsky's 1987 film *Falklands War: The Untold Story*. In this documentary footage, which is projected onto a large screen on stage in *Minefield*, the younger Lou appears visibly upset and shaken as he laments straight into the lens of the camera. Before the young Argentinian soldier passes away, he tells Lou in English that he once went to Oxford and confesses that he does not even know why he is fighting in the war. As Jordana Blejmar notes, 'The scene points to a moment of revelation for the British veteran, the moment in which the enemy acquired a face (and a voice), one that looked and spoke surprisingly like him' (2017: 115). The scene resonates with the final one of *Redacted*, Brian de Palma's film about the Iraq war, in which the character of the US war veteran McCoy makes a tearful confession when pressed by friends for 'war stories' during a 'Welcome Home' party in a bar. Like Lou, who confesses that he could never forget the face of the Argentine youth, McCoy admits that 'I have these snapshots in my brain that are burned in there forever, and I don't know what the fuck I'm going to do about them.'

In *Minefield*, Lou explains that he never attends veteran gatherings in his own country because, instead of shedding tears over lives lost by his compatriots, he still feels guilty for mourning the young Argentine who died in his arms. He also tells the audience about suffering from flashbacks, sleepless nights, and stress when rehearsing for *Minefield* in Buenos Aires and remembering the violence he had participated in during the war. His fellow British soldier David Jackson and the Argentine Marcelo Vallejo have offered similar testimonies, indicative of the fact that they all suffered from post-traumatic stress disorder (PTSD). Indeed, Marcelo's life after the war included a suicide attempt as well as alcohol and cocaine addictions. Like the previously discussed scene from *Minefield*, this one also runs the risk of re-wounding its narrator and the remaining cast members. They confirmed as much at a workshop that I attended with them in April 2018 at Home, a theatre venue in Manchester, after seeing their show there the night before. I would like to unpack this scene (as narrated by Lou, but also in a way by the rest of the show) by employing Robert Lifton's reflection on witnessing the Vietnam War, since his political rethinking of traumatic repetition is still relevant and of historical significance here.

In his book *Home from the War*, Lifton grapples with the significance of what he sees as the larger mission of bearing witness that many Vietnam veterans undertook on their return from the war. He describes the tasks of a returning Vietnam veteran in terms of the political and ethical 'truth mission' emerging from the Vietnam experience. His account draws on his own interactions with the veterans starting in 1970, during the war, when he and another psychiatrist led conversation groups where soldiers could explore the haunting images of their nightmares and flashbacks as well as their repetitive experiences of guilt and re-enactments. While these veterans used the term 'Vietnam Syndrome' in their testimonies, which was eventually replaced by 'Post-traumatic Stress Disorder', their use of it denoted not only a psychological pathology but equally so 'an attempt (if still unsuccessful) to bear witness to events that no one else wanted to see or hear' (Caruth 2017: 611). Lifton pays particular attention to the 'death imprint' left on the soldiers' minds by war's meaningless slaughter (1992: 11). In Lifton's view, the soldiers' anti-war interventions were closely linked to the urgency with which they witnessed Vietnam War's pervasive 'absurdity and antimeaning' (1992: 40).

Lifton also relates how the specific conditions of this war led many soldiers who encountered them to experience a breakdown in their sense of having a meaningful mission. Like the Falklands war veterans, the Vietnam war veterans testified to 'a sense of the war's total lack of order or structure, the feeling that there was no genuine purpose, that nothing could ever be secured or gained, and there could be no measurable progress' (Lifton 1992: 38). Due to 'an overall inability to give significant form – to formulate – one's war-linked death immersion' (Lifton 1992: 38–9), the soldiers faced a rupture in meaning on both an individual and a collective level. The veterans' attempts to transmit an image of atrocity in the war's aftermath should be seen not only in terms of psychological healing, or historical truth-telling, but also as political acts. Such attempts constituted witnessing acts that simultaneously transmitted and challenged the absurdity of the war.

The injunction to remember is linked perhaps to faith in the redressive capacities of memory, the founding distinction, or break, between then and now. But how might we understand mourning when the event has yet come to end? Mourning, as a public expression of one's grief, insists that the past is not yet over. Additionally, as Athena Athanasiou points out, 'the politics of mourning has always been premised upon gender, kinship, and national normativity' (2017: 1). Her book *Agonistic Mourning* looks at the antinationalist, feminist organization Women in Black (*Žene u crnom*), which was started by a group of Israeli Jewish and Palestinian women holding placards proclaiming 'End the Occupation' in 1988. The movement gradually spread from Israel/Palestine to include other feminist actions worldwide aimed against ethno-nationalist violence, militarism, imperialist power, capitalist injustices, racism, sexism, and homophobia. Women in Black emerged in Belgrade, Serbia (then Yugoslavia), in 1991 as part of the resistance against Slobodan Milošević and, more specifically, as a feminist critique of nationalism and militarism.

It organized weekly anti-war public actions from October 1991 to October 1995 at the Republic Square in Belgrade as well as commemorations at sites of past atrocities committed in the name of the nation. Mourning for the national 'other' – and generally mourning otherwise – constitutes the hallmark of Women in Black activism. According to Athanasiou (2017: 71), the movement 'undermines the normative role assigned to women by nationalism and kinship normativity by re-embodying the sign of mourning outside the sanctioned boundaries of proper femininity and national allegiance'.

In dialogue with scholars such as Jacques Derrida, Giorgio Agamben, and Judith Butler, Athanasiou raises a critical question of how kinship is mobilized to secure the conditions by which some lives become liveable and recognizable, while others are repudiated and foreclosed. It does so by constituting a social sphere where the differential production and allocation of grief and grievability operates, as Butler writes in *Precarious Life*, 'to produce and maintain certain exclusionary conceptions of who is normatively human: what counts as livable life and a grievable death?' (2004: xiv–xv).

In Butler's view, ethics is located not in the self but in one's compassionate response to the face of the other, which expresses their alterity. As she elaborates:

Perhaps most importantly, we must recognize that ethics requires us to risk ourselves precisely at moments of unknowingness, when what forms us diverges from what lies before us, when our willingness to become undone in relation to others constitutes our chance of becoming human. To be undone by another is a primary necessity, an anguish, to be sure, but also a chance – to be addressed, claimed, bound to what is not me, but also to be moved, to be prompted to act, to address myself elsewhere, and so to vacate the self-sufficient 'I' as a kind of possession. If we speak and try to give an account from this place, we will not be irresponsible, or, if we are, we will surely be forgiven. (2005: 136)

By bearing witness to unwitnessable lives and by mourning unmournable deaths, Lou's testimony signals a complex politics of mourning in which his claim to a right to mourn publicly registers also as a political grievance. His grief is thus not only an act of mourning the loss of the Other but simultaneously an act of repairing the Other – an act of reparation. His testimony becomes an occasion to witness both the finality of death and our own implication in the violent deaths of others. Indeed, the struggle to see, interpret, and face the consequences of bearing witness is central not just for Lou and the rest of the cast but also for the audience, which becomes increasingly implicated in the witnessing act through participation in the performance.

Arias considers the choice of using war veterans rather than professionally trained actors in the show as 'the most political thing about doing the documentary theatre' (qtd. in Bither 2019: n.p.). For such a cast, participating in a performance can provide insight into their own experiences and become a novel way of communicating with and about their own past. Additionally, such an experience allows them to encounter an audience of people they would not normally meet and to get their feedback and recognition. The veterans' agency in re-presenting the past, secured by the show's framework, 'is both a political and a humane act, a way of considering how empathy functions and where spaces of difference might remain between the different combatants' (Delgado 2019: 14). Perhaps surprisingly given its title, Arias succeeds in creating such a shared site of encounter in *Minefield*, a space 'where self and other engage in a dialogue between a lived past, an enacted present and an imagined future' (Delgado 2019: 13) and where we can still envision people meeting and getting along, coexisting peacefully, cooperating, and living in a state of mutual aid and moral solidarity – a common ground of sorts.

Case Study 2: Yael Ronen's *Common Ground*

Created in 2015 by Ronen and her actors at the Maxim Gorki theatre in Berlin, *Common Ground* started out as a meditation on the aftermath of the war in the former Yugoslavia. That same year, the performance was invited to the renowned Theatertreffen Festival in Berlin and won the audience award at the Mülheimer Theatertage. Its director, born in Jerusalem in 1976 and currently working as an in-house director at the Gorki theatre, is internationally recognized as one of the most exciting theatre makers of her generation. Ronen's productions often employ black humour in the framework of historical conflicts. Ten years ago, along with an ensemble of Israeli, German, and Palestinian actors, she produced *Third Generation* (*Dritte Generation* 2009), which premiered at the Schaubühne in Berlin and in Tel Aviv shortly thereafter. The show became a huge European success as well as sparked heated debates. Since it premiered, thousands of people from the Middle East have arrived in Berlin and around a million in Germany, a change that prompted Ronen to revisit the material with another production: *Third Generation – Next Generation* (Gorki 2019), featuring both people from Arab countries and Israelis. Ronen was also recognized for *The Situation* (Gorki 2015), a performance that negotiated the political situation in the Middle East and which was selected by critics as the play of 2016 in the annual survey by *Theater heute* journal. She also directed *Winterreise* with the newly founded Exil Ensemble at the Gorki (2017), receiving the fourteenth Europe Prize for Theatrical Realities that same year.

As mentioned earlier, the cast of *Common Ground* comprised mainly of actors who originally came from the territories of the former Yugoslavia and settled in Berlin in the 1990s, either as refugees or as second-generation Con migrants. The performance documents both the actors' research trip to Bosnia and Herzegovina and their impressions of, and reflections on, the current situation there. Their memories of life in the ex-Yugoslavia during the breakup of the country are also at play in *Common Ground*. During the production process, as Stephen Wilmer documents, the actors 'discovered uncanny coincidences about their family circumstances that awakened dark memories, such as one actor's father having been killed in a prison where another actor's father had worked' (2018: 83). Its predominantly documentary genealogy notwithstanding, Ronen notes that there were elements of artifice in the performance: the actors would sometimes 'put a little bit more of an artistic disguise on it or fictional disguise in order to create also some kind of common layer of protection' (qtd. in Wilmer 2018: 83).

In Berlin, the play could find an audience comprising of members of immigrant communities as well as of Berliners, and certainly life in a host country which is a powerful neoliberal nation is acutely under investigation. The production was also shown at the International Theatre Festival (MESS) in Sarajevo, however, with audiences there responding to different stakes and exhibiting a different degree of intimacy and recognition. I recorded my initial impressions of the performance in an email exchange with Janelle Reinelt:

These young people are children of victims and perpetrators – though in the main narrative the victims are always only Bosnian Muslims and the perpetrators Bosnian Serbs ... The play was performed in the National Theatre in downtown Sarajevo to standing ovations. But I wonder what would happen if the performance was presented in the National Theatre in Banja Luka – the capital of the Republic of Srpska, in Bosnia and Herzegovina, with a predominantly Serbian population. Still I thought this was a powerful performance although its politics could be questioned and contested. Does it work on reconciliation, co-habitation, mutual recognition etc. – hardly – in my view. The microcosm of the performance does not fully, productively, and justly reflect the larger issues related to the civil war and the current stakes and issues in Bosnian politics and life today. (From personal mail, 20 October 2015)

I remember appreciating at that time the experience of trying to reconstruct our collective tragedy, the opportunity to revisit the familiar auditorium of the National theatre nearly two decades since my last visit, and the proximity of an audience that shares my sense of humour. Still, I could not fully relate to the narrative presented, in part because all atrocities enumerated in the work were committed only by one – the Serbian – side of the conflict. From my perspective, the reality of the Bosnian civil war still seems infinitely more complex than the performance suggested.

While the epilogue to the Bosnian political crisis is yet to be written, the performance supports Norman Naimark's observation that the key problem standing in the way of plural cohabitation in Bosnia is that of identity. Naimark draws some sombre conclusions after an international conference dedicated to the tenth anniversary of the genocide in Srebrenica that took place in Sarajevo in 2005. He argues that, like the other two main ethnic groups in Bosnia and Herzegovina, Bosniaks strive to develop 'their own national institutions and culture, based primarily on their identity as victims', while simultaneously advocating the dissolution of ethnically based institutional arrangements inherited from Dayton in exchange for 'a united, democratic, and multi-national Bosnia-Herzegovina' (2009: 16). For this historian, the main obstacle for the country and its future is perpetuating the narrative of Bosniaks' victimhood at the hands of the Serbs while simultaneously seeking 'to incorporate a substantial Serbian population into the new Bosnia-Herzegovina', to which he adds 'similar, but less vital questions about the Croats' (2009: 16). Naimark concludes, 'If the genocide is at the core of national consciousness, then it is hard to imagine [that] a multi-national state can succeed in the future. But there are no workable alternatives' (2009: 18).

Naimark's observations from a decade ago unfortunately still largely hold for present-day Bosnia Herzegovina. As this book's introduction relates, the most recent controversy, which erupted after the Austrian writer Peter Handke was announced as a winner of the 2019 Nobel Prize in Literature on 10 October, demonstrates that these narratives – dropped by the rest of the world in favour of ever-new conflicts on the horizon – have never achieved closure. They are still being repeated. Nonetheless, from the distance of the years that passed since I saw the performance, I am more drawn to explore the psychic complexities represented in this performance of what it means to survive and to inherit, however indirectly, traumatic events that fail to be recognized and worked through over many years; of what it means to live with the dead, and how these performed testimonies can act as modes of repair, with repair understood here largely as intrapsychic process rather than an ethical, political, and legal concept.

In parallel to the long development process that Lola Arias and her cast went through in working on *Minefield*, Ronen and her actors faced their share of challenges while probing memory's illusive nature. Ronen recalls some of the difficulties of combining theatre and real life:

> There is one fight that is the most loud fight on stage that we have that really happened and when it happened in real life it was very emotional and people were crying ... There were also a lot of very emotional fights and breakdowns ... We really had to ... take the responsibility of one step beyond creating a play, but really taking care of a very vulnerable group of people that are handling very deep wounds ... A play kind of erupted out of a very personal group therapy process. (qtd. in Wilmer 2018: 82).

Drawing on these recollections as well as interviews with people they met during their trip to Bosnia and Herzegovina, *Common Ground* begins in 1991, progressing swiftly through Yugoslavia's chaotic and devastating subsequent collapse from there. The stage is set by two onlookers – Nahmias from Israel (who could also be seen as a stand-in for the director Ronen) and Bormann, a German actor – who explain how they all came together to share their experiences and stories. The company creates an overlapping collage of the 1990s, with the civil war in Bosnia and Herzegovina and the NATO military intervention in Serbia in 1999 set against a backdrop of global shifts. After speeding through a chronology of events, such as the siege of Sarajevo, the destruction of the old Ottoman bridge in Mostar, and the NATO bombing of the Federal Republic of Yugoslavia (FRY) in 1999, the actors begin the difficult process of piecing together their personal and collective pasts. Surrounded by the debris of Magda Willi's design – all boxes and clutter – they engage in a slow and arduous process of rebuilding both literally and figuratively. They stack and slot portions of the set together, trying new combinations, thereby mirroring the process of these 'new' Berliners coming together to share experiences marked by similar guilt and blame and to compare conflicting narratives – indeed, mirroring the show itself.

When the company visited Bosnia and Herzegovina, the people they met often found it difficult to talk about what happened two decades earlier. As one Sarajevo resident put it, the war never really ended: it continued within people, poisonously unresolved. These challenges were perhaps nowhere more manifest than in a scene between the collective and Bakira Hasečić, a war and rape survivor of the Bosnian conflict. Hasečić lived in the eastern Bosnian town of Višegrad during the conflict, in an area subject to ethnic cleansing in 1992. After the war, she became one of the most prominent human rights campaigners in Bosnia and Herzegovina, founding the Association for Women Victims of War and testifying at the International Criminal Tribunal for the former Yugoslavia in The Hague. The meeting between the cast of *Common Ground* and Hasečić took place in a small office in Sarajevo, where she works to collect and preserve the testimonies of the conflict's female survivors. She told her story through an interpreter, Aleksandar, a company member of Serbian descent born in Belgrade, who translated it for the German and

Israeli members of the ensemble. A large video projection of Hasečić's testimony is played in a slow motion on stage when Aleksandar describes this testimonial encounter during the performance. 'The room is full of smoke. Bakira chain-smokes. As if she couldn't breathe without a cigarette', says Aleksandar, before he starts retelling the traumatic experiences of Hasečić's multiple rapes and the massacre of her neighbours.

When I saw this scene in the auditorium of the National Theatre in Sarajevo, I became aware of the multiple layers of time at play in this encounter: the temporal distance between the horrific violence she suffered during the war, her testimony at the ICTY, and finally its retelling in *Common Ground*. Trauma travels through space and time, from survivor to actor to audience, refusing easy translation. This particular scene conveys something that 'factical' court transcripts, media reports, and scholarly discourse analysis almost inevitably fail to do. While it is important to honour the achievements of recently created institutions like the International Commission for Human Rights and the International Criminal Court, it is also important to think what these institutional responses cannot achieve for recovering persons, communities, and nations, as Jill Stauffer notes. She contests the belief that criminal trials and truth commissions are cathartic, or healing, for survivors, and that criminal accountability or the 'truth' of such commissions facilitates political reconciliation. Recognizing that legal trials and truth commissions both respond to repair past harms, Stauffer nevertheless finds that 'punishing a perpetrator does not rebuild the selves and worlds destroyed by human rights abuses, and so the retributive approach may leave entire communities' experiences of harm unaddressed' (2015: 41). Drawing on studies utilizing data from South Africa, Sierra Leone, Rwanda, and the former Yugoslavia, she argues that 'if trials aren't combined with other, more reparative efforts at the state or community level, most victims will not benefit in meaningful ways from international criminal cases' (2015: 45). A similar sentiment can be heard in Eric Stover's interpretation of what testifying did for witnesses in the ICTY cases:

Human rights activists often valorise the 'therapeutic value' of war crimes trials for victims and witnesses. They argue that victims who are able to recount horrific events in a context of acknowledgement and support will often find closure and be able to move on with their lives. The findings of this study (and corroborating data from our parallel studies ...), however, suggest that such claims so far as war crimes trials are concerned reflect more wishful thinking than fact. The few participants who experienced cathartic feelings immediately or soon after testifying before the ICTY found that the glow quickly faded once they returned home to their shattered villages and towns. This was especially true for witnesses who faced uncertainties in their lives. (2004: 107)

Many analyses of the experience of women testifying before the South African TRC likewise show that the effect of testimonies generated through the truth commission, media, and academics did not necessarily make a difference in these subjects' recovery.

All of this points to a site of repair outside the victim-perpetrator continuum. One example is the Women's Court for the Balkans, a truth-seeking initiative initiated by local civil society organizations from all over the post-Yugoslav space (*Ženski Sud* n.d.), which took place in Sarajevo, Bosnia, and Herzegovina, from 4–7 May 2015. This court highlighted the various forms of structural violence that accompanied the 1990s conflicts in the region and the ways the latter specifically affected women (Women's Court 2011: 14). Besides the interethnic and interpersonal violence that are usually underlined, the court also highlighted the economic and social consequences of the conflict. Consequently, it was able to bring out the interconnectedness of various forms of violence and their continuity from wartime into the present, while questioning neoliberal capitalism, especially in respect to gendered and racialized regimes of socio-economic precarity.

As many scholars working on reconciliation issues argue, the responsibility for justice and recovery is not just a narrow legal concern but the very broadest of obligations. If reconciliation, transition, or peaceful cohabitation are to last, those having the luck of relative safety and security will need to perform revisionary practices on themselves in order to see that they are implicated both in the destruction of worlds and in the responsibility to rebuild them. We all have a job to do to create the conditions where repair is possible. Since selves and worlds are built through human interactions, however, some conditions make positive revisions more likely, while others do the reverse. Recovery may be easier for someone with broad social support than it is for someone like Hasečić, who has survived brutal treatment but comes from a community where her harms have not been addressed or widely recognized or are dismissed as part of a past that should be buried. In a recent interview for *The Herald*, Hasečić recalls returning to her hometown after the war 'only to find that men who had raped and murdered in the town were living and working there – many of them as police officers' (qtd. in Flockhart 2018: n.p.).

There is a sense here of being forced into 'ethical loneliness', as Stauffer describes, 'the isolation one feels when one, as a violated person or as one member of a persecuted group, has been abandoned by humanity' (2015: 1). The surrounding world exacerbates the individual's feeling of having been forsaken by turning a blind eye to the atrocity by failing to stop it or to acknowledge it. Ethical loneliness is the result of being forsaken not once but twice: 'the experience of having been abandoned by humanity compounded by the experience of not being heard' (Stauffer 2015: 1). Using many examples and contexts, Stauffer illustrates how careful listening and creating better conditions for listening is essential to re-establishing trust and community after serious violence. While Stauffer's book is primarily about the double abandonment and existential isolation experienced by Holocaust survivors and black South Africans under Apartheid, her argument for the fundamental importance of listening is equally relevant in the context of Bosnia and Herzegovina and the story Hasečić tells in *Common Ground*.

How may this encounter with the past fuel emancipatory efforts beyond those of contemplating the injury or apportioning blame for it? Can an act of witnessing counter the disavowals constitutive of the divided national community of Bosnia and Herzegovina? Is there any necessary relation between this act of remembrance and the act of redress? According to Dori Laub, the testimonial process requires 'a bonding, the intimate and total presence of an other – in the position of one who hears' (1992: 72). This intimacy is all too easy to ward off, however. Laub warns that, in trying too hard to bond, we may give in to 'a flood of awe and fear; we endow the survivor with a kind of sanctity, both to pay our tribute to him and to keep him at a distance, to avoid the intimacy entailed in knowing' (1992: 72). A similar dynamic is perceptible in the encounter between Aleksander and Hasečić, with the former being beset by contradictory feelings while trying to be a good listener, to be hospitable, and to acclimatize his listening (and interpreting) self to the most painful and unimaginable conditions of torture and trauma.

Aleksandar is ashamed of the violence Hasečić suffered in the hands of Serbian paramilitaries while also feeling judged by the rest of the Maxim Gorki collective on stage. He wonders about the wartime Serbian losses, wounds, and grievances: 'I feel betrayed and alone. I envy the victim position. In my head, I go through all massacres of Serbs that happened during the war. I want Orit and Tim to hear the horror stories about what happened to us', he says. This identificatory and potentially apologetic stance, however, is countered in the performance with moments of ideological contamination and implication. 'How have I become a "side" in this war?' asks Aleksandar as he searches for his German passport, as if locating this marker of his new national allegiance and identity can make history's burden evaporate.

What the scene also points to is the binary nature of the oppositions that populate both sides (or rather three sides, including the Croats) of the Bosnian civil war narrative. As in the case of Israeli/Palestinian conflict, 'Each side is convinced that it is history's ultimate victim, while denying or downplaying the suffering of the other side in order to validate its own claim' (Bashir and Amos, qtd. in Rothberg 2019: 121). The scene in question is far from being 'an ugly contest of comparative victimization' (Rothberg 2009: 7), however, or an arbitrary conjunction of two separate histories. Instead, it contains an important insight into the dynamics of collective memory and the struggles over recognition and collective identity that continue to haunt present-day Bosnia and Herzegovina.

For the audience, the affect generated by this scene of bearing witness to the sufferings of others and, by extension, to one's own implication in those sufferings involves an empathic connection with the feelings of the witness-sufferer. Dori Laub's influential take on the theory of dialogic traumatic witnessing posits that the witness to trauma testimony 'comes to feel the bewilderment, injury, confusion, dread and conflicts that the trauma victim feels. He has to address all these, if he is to carry out his function as a listener, and if trauma is to emerge, so that its henceforth impossible witnessing can indeed take place' (1992: 58).

The scene is dense with historically specific detail as well as personal, generational, ethnic, and local differences, which inevitably modulate any binary simplifications.

Michael Rothberg's notion of the 'implicated subject', which articulates how legacies of violence reside in us across space, time, and generation, illuminates what is morally, ethically, and politically at stake here. Drawing inspiration in part from Hanna Arendt's claim that we lack adequate concepts for describing what she called 'this vicarious responsibility for things we have not done' (qtd. in Rothberg 2019: 1), Rothberg argues that the most often invoked figures – of victims, perpetrators, and bystanders – cannot fully explain our connection to injustices past and present. In the figure of the implicated subject, Rothberg offers a new theory of political responsibility. It is a category that 'serves as an umbrella term that gathers a range of subject positions that sit uncomfortably in our familiar conceptual space of victims, perpetrators, and bystanders' (2019: 13). The need for it stems from the fact that '[m]odes of implication – entanglement in historical and present day injustices – are complex, multifaceted, and sometimes contradictory, but … nonetheless essential to confront in the pursuit of justice' (Rothberg 2019: 2). The lens of implication allows us to address these different scales and temporalities of injustice. Furthermore, the framework of implicated subjects opens up a space for new coalitions of identities and groups to come together by drawing attention to shared responsibilities for violence and injustice while diverging from the discourse of guilt (which fosters denial and defensiveness in proximity to ongoing conflicts) to situate accountability in 'a less legally and emotionally charged terrain of historical and political responsibility' (Rothberg 2019: 20).

Rothberg uses the concept of the implicated subject to address situations where contemporary and historical problems of responsibility intersect, as exemplified by the complicated legacies of the Holocaust, racial slavery in the United States, the South African apartheid, and the persistent crisis of Israel/Palestine. An approach based on implication can be also useful, however, in illuminating heterogeneous cases of historical and contemporary violence and injustice, as presented in *Common Ground* as a whole and particularly the scene under discussion. Clearly, the sources of such implication are different from those underpinning the legacies of slavery and settler colonialism. Here, it is less a matter of being a 'beneficiary' and more the case of Aleksander's ideological interpellation as a Serb into relation with Serbia (his homeland) and the Republic of Srpska (one of two political entities in the Bosnia and Herzegovina), along with the affective bonds that accompany such interpellation. Although the scene presents Aleksander as a vulnerable subject – we find out later in the performance that he was born in Belgrade in 1985 and was still a child during the Bosnian conflict, including the NATO air strikes on the city in 1999 – it does not entirely exonerate him. Rather, the scene underscores a subject-position that contains elements of both victimization and perpetration and in this way articulates a sense of transgenerational implication.

By presenting Aleksander as an implicated subject, *Common Ground* challenges the very possibility of a historically innocent subject position at the intersection of individual experience and transgenerational collective legacy. The audience is at once drawn in and kept at bay, facing a constellation of irresolution and implication that resolutely refutes easy negotiations with the past. The scene's moving power springs in part from its invitation for spectators to take up divergent positions towards those commemorated on stage and to bear diverse affective burdens, including grief (in the case of empathic witnessing by proxy) and guilt (if stirred to acknowledge, or bear witness to, their own, possibly unintentional implication in a tragic past). Responding to this scene means bearing some form of responsibility and recognizing ourselves in the position of the implicated subject. On the night that I saw this performance, the spectators in the National Theatre auditorium must have felt a wide range of degrees of implication between them. Many of them would probably also agree, as I do, with Rothberg's assessment that the necessity of revising the past means that 'the confrontation with historical violence is ongoing, its expiration date uncertain' (2019: 20).

The show's final scene nevertheless gestures, however tentatively, at the emergence of a progressive, bottom-up political mobilization involving all three main national constituencies in Bosnia and Herzegovina. In it, one of the actors, Vernesa, first reflects on her pervading sense of alienation from her homeland, which remains largely divided along the ethnic and religious lines more than two decades after the Dayton Peace Accord was signed (in 1995): 'I went to Bosnia as a tourist for the first time. For the first time, as I'm leaving, I have the feeling that Bosnia is no longer mine' (Ronen et al. 2014: 63). She explains further: 'The Republika Srpska is almost ethnically cleansed of Bosniaks. The Bosnian Federation is almost ethnically cleansed of Serbs. Serbia is almost ethnically cleansed of Croats. Croatia is almost ethnically cleansed of Serbs. And everyone feels like shit' (Ronen et al. 2014: 63–4). She also comments on the social uprisings of February 2014, a watershed moment in the history of Bosnia and Herzegovina:

> The day we leave Bosnia demonstrations begin. Bosnian Muslims, Serbs and Croats – all angry together against the government structure. They demand to be able to live with dignity, work and an end to the corruption. In the news, they show the demonstrators waving three flags: Bosnian, Serbian and Croatian. It gives me hope. As though Tito's old motto 'brotherhood and unity' had new relevance. (Ronen et al. 2014: 64)

The protests referenced here were sparked by frustrated workers in Tuzla, an eastern Bosnian city with a long history of labour movements. Its people took to the streets in huge numbers to voice their discontent with an unaccountable political elite, to oppose the privatization of factories, which left many of them unemployed, and to lament the worsening of living conditions. As the police reacted to the escalation of tensions with force, citizens and workers all over the country joined the demonstrations while international news outlets flashed images of burning buildings. The protestors' demands quickly broadened to include calls for the resignation of governments at cantonal, entity, and state levels. The significance of these protests for my analysis is twofold: one, they enacted a potent critique of the liberal transition model established in Bosnia with the support of international organizations after the civil war (1992–5); and two, while the crucial concerns of protesters were socioeconomic, these events were also strongly linked to the war and wartime violence. This moment of civil unrest in Bosnia's post-war stasis is thus also instructive for future visions of how reconciliation and repair can take place in this country.

To understand the political economy of the 2014 protests, they must be situated in the broader context of long-term, structural socio-economic reforms that were implemented in the former Yugoslav state after the collapse of the socialist system. Unlike its neighbours and former members of Yugoslavia who are the new or brand-new members of the European Union, or current candidates for membership in it, Bosnia and Herzegovina is the only post-Yugoslav state with the status of a potential candidate for EU membership. As a result, Bosnia and Herzegovina has to abide by the rules and conditions set forth by the EU, the International Monetary Fund (IMF), and the World Bank. The economic reforms in the areas of privatization, labour laws, and welfare, which reshaped the previous socialist economy in neoliberal terms, did not redress the everyday forms of socioeconomic violence that Bosnian people suffered during the war, however. Instead, the neoliberal restructuring of the country aggravated the situation, bringing about a further decline in living standards for a population already ravaged by four years of violent conflict. The transition process progressively impoverished the Bosnian-Herzegovinian citizens, heightening social inequalities to the extent of eliminating the middle class and bringing the working class to the brink of existence. It was the social groups that were most affected by the consequences of neoliberal reforms, such as workers, pensioners, the unemployed, the laid-off, as well as the precariously employed, who took to the streets to express their anger at their government and the international community, with both blamed for embracing a reform programme that plundered their factories and degraded their living standards further.

One characteristic of the 2014 protests was their rejection of ethnicity as a form of identification, which represented a radical response to the rigid ethno-nationalist frameworks of political participation typical of the Bosnian system. As Slavoj Žižek wrote for *The Guardian* in February 2014, some of the slogans that appeared during the demonstrations exemplified the importance given to socioeconomic issues over those of ethnicity:

In one of the photos of the protests, we see the demonstrators waving three flags side by side: Bosnian, Serb, Croat, expressing the will to ignore ethnic differences. In short, we are dealing with the rebellion against nationalist elites: the people of Bosnia have finally understood who their true enemy is: not other ethnic groups, but their own leaders who pretend to protect them from others. It is as if the old and much-abused Titoist motto of the 'brotherhood and unity' of Yugoslav nations acquired new actuality. (2014)

The notion of Yugoslavian unity was thus evoked not nostalgically but deliberately, as a sign of protest that acquired a clear anti-capitalist dimension. Furthermore, all citizens regardless of their nationality and religion were invited to take part in the process of debating and developing the protesters' claims. City after city, democratic assemblies called 'plenums' were formed, echoing in their name the political assemblies from communist times. They were defined, however, as 'public gatherings, open to any citizen, through which collective decisions and demands can be made and action taken beyond guarantees of leadership. They are open, direct, and transparent democracy in practice' (Arsenijević 2014: 47–8).

These initiatives became a way of regionally and transnationally connecting intellectuals, students, and activists united around the struggles for social justice and the insistence on a politics of memory, anti-fascism, commonality, and solidarity under galloping capitalism. Direct democracy and the creation of social resistance on the street by grassroots citizens' associations and leaderless movements across Bosnia and Herzegovina in 2014 have also given way to expressing the political in non-traditional ways, going beyond nationalist options on offer by parliamentary parties in the country, while bringing to the fore the conflictual nature of democracy, or what the ancient Greeks called *stasis*, which, to Dimitris Vardoulakis, 'is the definitional characteristic of democracy *and* of any other possible constitutional form' (2018: 11, his emphasis).

Recent political theory has seen a resurgence of interest in the notion of 'stasis', as apparent from the Nazi jurist Carl Schmitt's *Political Theology II* (1970) – a lesser – known companion to his famous *Political Theology I* (1922) – and Nicole Loraux's *Divided City* (2002), to Giorgio Agamben's *Stasis: Civil War as a Political Paradigm* (2015) and Dimitris Vardoulakis' *Stasis Before the State* (2018). At the same time, the global spread of popular anti-establishment uprisings against neoliberal governance has brought the notions of civil war and revolt – both of them included in the semantic field of stasis – to the forefront of contemporary political debates. It would be impossible to elucidate here all of the ramifications of these authors' complex arguments concerning stasis. For the purposes of my analysis here, I will briefly relate Agamben's key reflections on the concept while also linking his work to that of Vardoulakis.

In *Stasis: Civil War as Political Paradigm*, Agamben discusses the role of stasis, or civil strife, at two paradigmatic moments in Western political thought: the time of ancient Greece and the 1651 publication of Hobbes' *Leviathan*. Agamben argues that both instances reveal stasis to be a contradictory phenomenon that poses a threat to the existing order while also being necessary for its re-establishment. As he puts it, the notion of stasis 'constitutes a zone of indifference between the unpolitical space of the family and the political space of the city' (2015: 12). For Agamben, 'in Greek politics civil war functions as a threshold of politicisation and depoliticisation' (2015: 12), where the alliances commanded by the realms of family and city, *oikos* and polis, clash and contaminate each other. Stasis (fratricidal war) turns the members of the same polis (the same political family) into enemies and ruptures existing family bonds to create new political alliances. While seeing fratricidal war as a dangerous misfortune, Greek culture exemplifies an attitude that tries to negotiate the extremes of politicization and depoliticization instead of simply rejecting stasis. At one end of the spectrum stands Solon's law (from the early sixth century BCE) that designates 'the citizen who had not fought for either one of the two sides in a civil war' (2015: 12) as punishable with the loss of civil rights. Refusing to participate in a civil war, therefore, amounts 'to being expelled from the *polis* and confined to the *oikos*' (2015: 13). On the other end of the spectrum is the law of amnesty, which mandated that past divisions within the polis be forgotten after the cessation of hostilities. Agamben refers here to a watershed moment in 403 BCE when the first amnesty in the history of politics was offered. After their inglorious defeat during the Peloponnesian war and their subsequent overthrow of the dictatorship of the Thirty and victorious return of the democrats to the city, Athenians call for an amnesty: that is, they call for a forgetting of the past so as to guarantee the stability and unity of the polis. They agreed to forget the unforgettable, namely the civil strife, in favour of their city's stability. Per Agamben according to Aristotle: 'From the juridical point of view, *stasis* thus seems to be defined by two prohibitions, which perfectly cohere with one another: on the one hand, not participating in it is politically culpable; on the other, forgetting it once it has finished is a political duty' (2015: 15). Rather provocatively, this is 'just the opposite, that is to say, of what civil war seems to be for the moderns: namely, something that one must seek to render impossible at every cost, yet that must always be remembered through trials and legal prosecutions' (2015: 16).

Like Agamben, Vardoulakis underscores the democratic potential of stasis. He discusses the mentioned Solon's law, arguing that the fundamental political distinction for a radical democracy is not between friend and enemy – 'us' and 'them' – but between *active* and *passive* citizenship. In Agamben's view, Solon's law might seem counterintuitive and even shocking today. In Vardoulakis' interpretation, however, the law does not promote violence and animosity among citizens but simply declares that during an acute political crisis, neutrality is politically, ethically, and legally unacceptable: 'Solon's law describes not only the state in which one is – active or inactive – but also indicates that one ought to be active at the cost of losing their citizenship' (2018: 69). When the polis is in turmoil, only the state of generalized unrest holds the potential of future peace.

The first transitional justice interventions in the former Yugoslavia (as well as internationally) were characterized by a top-down establishment of international institutions that generally focused on criminal accountability, such as the International Criminal Tribunal for the former Yugoslavia (ICTY), which was the first international tribunal to be established after the International Military Tribunal in Nuremberg. Such institutions face considerable limitations when tackling complex justice demands in post-war contexts, which soon became apparent also in the case of former Yugoslavia. Their key contribution is fighting against impunity after mass atrocities and consolidating international principles of accountability, but retributive transitional justice often leaves out other crucial considerations, for instance, of the social inequalities and structural discriminations that may have provoked the violence and could continue unabated even after the 'transition'. Legal institutions such as the ICTY can do little to reinforce domestic legal systems or to address issues of socioeconomic justice, the reconciliation process, and social change. The crisis in Bosnia and Herzegovina in 2014 revealed many of these contradictions. The protests and 'plenum' assemblies of citizens 'envisaged redistributive policies and changes in the political and economic model of the country as the primary way of redressing the dire conditions faced by Bosnian people' (Lai and Bonora 2019: 56).

The protests in question also effectively highlighted the socioeconomic violence experienced in many Bosnian cities during the conflict, turning it into a public and political issue for the first time since the end of the war. When the international community promoted reconciliation between formerly opposed ethnic groups after the war, it completely ignored the legacy of (socioeconomic) wartime violence and its consequences for the post-war period: industry reduced to a fraction of its prewar capacity, frequent overlap between acts of ethnic cleansing and theft, loss of employment due to ethnic discrimination, along with other measures of social exclusion. Such experiences constituted a major part of people's lives during and after the war. As Branislav Jakovljevic writes, 'Wars destroy lives, but at the same time they produce societies built precisely on crimes and injustices of wartime violence. A thorough pacification of a post-war society is the perpetuation of that destruction by other means' (2018: 212). In February 2014, a multitude of citizens of Bosnia and Herzegovina demonstrated that repression of this past is a politically unproductive form of amnesty. In standing together instead of taking sides, these political actors embodied the polis in ways that echo what Agamben has described as a 'divided city' – one constituted on the basis of that which it disavows. By protesting, the people spoke against a form of forgetting that benefits only the ethno-oligarchs and tycoons who took over the country's economy in the post-war period by buying up businesses and factories at severely reduced prices while using the war to erase the traces of this plunder of communal property.

Srećko Horvat and Igor Štiks, in reflecting on the mass protests in Bosnia and many others that have taken place in Serbia, Croatia, Slovenia, Bosnia, Montenegro, and Macedonia over the past several years, described this political moment as follows:

> In their efforts to defend the remnants of the socialist state (primarily in education and health), natural and social resources (water, electricity, internet), and jobs (remaining industries, the public sector), they also begun to formulate a profoundly anti-capitalist and radically democratic vision of their societies. This is how radical politics was reborn in the rebel peninsula. (2014: 2)

In other words, a common struggle in Bosnia and Herzegovina (and other republics of the former Yugoslavia) is possible if we focus on finding a common ground in existing struggles. As Silvija Jestrović writes:

They demonstrate the strategy of doing Leftist politics-in-small-steps, which has the capacity to include other issues that emerge in our time in addition to those of workers' rights and union struggles, struggles in the region that oppose privatisation of the commons and public goods like water, forests, agricultural land, a factories, healthcare, education, urban public spaces, public transportation and other infrastructure. (2019: 7)

International actors have largely failed to understand the nature of these protests and their connection to the legacy of the war, pushing for a programme of economic reforms that follows the blueprint of previous attempts at liberalizing the market and completing the privatization process instead. What the crisis showed is that civic mobilization was indeed possible in Bosnia and Herzegovina, as is entertaining progressive debates on the future of the country. While the structural problems affecting Bosnia have not been solved, the protests have fostered the grassroots mobilization of citizens united in solidarity across social divisions and ethnic lines. In so doing, they have shown what a potentially transformative mobilization for post-war social justice might look like. Finally, the protests saw 'the emergence of a new collective identity no longer grounded in ethnicity, but rather deprivation' (Milan 2017: 169); time will tell whether this new encompassing subjectivity will be able to supplant the ethno-national divide.

Case Study 3: Robert Lepage's
The Seven Streams of the River Ota

In his seminal study entitled *Untimely Interventions*, Ross Chambers hypothesizes that 'events and experiences that are traumatic, whether collectively or to individuals, and become the object of witnessing practices have the cultural status of the obscene' (2004: 23). Chambers defines the obscene as 'the "offstage" or "backstage" space that delimits, and is simultaneously inseparable from, a scene of activity on which attention is focused. The cultural obscene is "obscured" or "covered" with respect to a scene of culture, but without being discontinuous with it' (2004: 23). Robert Lepage's *The Seven Streams of the River Ota* (1994–8), this chapter's last case study, brings the obscene – as Chambers defines it – onto the cultural stage to serve as a (often unwelcome) wake-up call for a culture that would rather ignore the traumatic histories and narratives evoked by the obscene. Lepage's performance weaves together the often disavowed traumatic experiences and events of the Hiroshima and Nagasaki atomic bombings, the Holocaust, and the AIDS crisis in unpredictable new ways, unleashing and placing centre-stage a torrent of voices, images, and ghosts that refuse historical closure.

While *The Seven Streams of the River Ota* was created to commemorate the fiftieth anniversary of the atomic bombings of Hiroshima and Nagasaki, it also addresses the Holocaust and the AIDS crisis of the 1980s and the 1990s. Most of the stage action unfolds in Hiroshima, with some scenes taking place in Osaka, Amsterdam, Terezín, and New York. Ric Knowles described the production as a 'kind of interculturalist "six degrees of separation"' which 'brings together disasters and healings that range from Hiroshima to the Holocaust to AIDS and explores, not causal or even analogical relations between them but their interrelated impact on a group of people related through blood, friendship, and history' (2000: 91–2). Emerging from Lepage's collaboration with *Ex Machina*, his permanent Quebec-based company, the production was his most ambitious undertaking at that time. It involved twenty-three co-producing organizations and was over seven hours long in its final form (Fricker 2020: 233). As Karen Fricker notes, the version presented and published in 1996 (which she edited) was originally intended to represent the end of the creative process, but Lepage and his collaborators kept working on the show into 1997, with this later version subsequently influenced by their work on a short film directed by Francis Leclerc 'in which each of the production's seven sections was distilled into seven minutes' (Fricker 2020: 248). One key difference between the earlier and later versions of the work concerns the character of Hanako, who is introduced as a child witnessing the nuclear blast over Hiroshima (which blinds her) at the beginning of both Leclerc's short film and the 1997 stage version. In the previous versions, Hanako had been introduced as the wife of the character Jeffrey Yamashita, whereas here she becomes his sister and Nozomi's daughter. Using the frame of Hanako's experiences from childhood through adulthood gave the overall production 'a strong narrative backbone connected to a single character's journey' (Fricker 2020: 248–9).

The actor-creators play several dozen characters in *The Seven Streams of the River Ota*, and all are linked by a complicated web of relationships that add up to the work's non-linear and modular narrative. The performance opens with a prologue stating that the production concerns 'people from different parts of the world who came to Hiroshima and found themselves confronted with their own devastation and their own enlightenment' (Lepage 1996: 1). (I am discussing here the version first performed in Quebec City on 17 May 1996 and published in 1996.) Part 1, 'Moving Pictures', begins with a brief affair between a US Army photographer named Luke O'Connor and Nozomi Yamashita, a disfigured survivor of the atomic bomb. Luke's mission is to document the damage to buildings and property in the now occupied Japan, but Nozomi asks him to turn his camera on her so that she can see what she looks like, since her mother-in-law had destroyed all mirrors in the house, as she explains. Luke thus has to witness a living example of the 'physical damage' caused by the nuclear blast in Nozomi's disfigurement (Lepage 1996: 3). This moment is rendered with sensitivity, as we never see Nozomi's face, nor are we shown the pictures that Luke subsequently takes of her wearing a beautiful kimono. At the end of part 1, before they part, Nozomi gives Luke a wedding doll to take home to his young son in Texas, which is to bring him a good wife when he grows up. We meet Luke's son, Jeffrey O'Connor (Jeffrey 1), in part 2, entitled 'Two Jeffreys', as he is seen caring for his father, who is dying from radiation-induced leukaemia, in a rundown New York apartment. The second Jeffrey refers to the offspring of Luke's romantic encounter with Nozomi twenty years earlier, now a young Japanese jazz musician named Jeffrey Yamashita (Jeffrey 2), who goes to New York after his mother's death to make contact with his father and half-brother. This part eventually culminates in a bittersweet recognition scene, when Jeffrey 2 reveals his true identity by giving his half-brother a photograph of their late father.

The play's third part moves the action forward by twenty years, as Jeffrey 1 comes to Amsterdam dying of AIDS to ask his old friend Ada Weber if she will marry him so that he can gain access to the Dutch-assisted suicide programme. Ada eventually consents to his request and this part ends with his suicide in an Amsterdam clinic, at which Jeffrey 2 is also present. Towards the end of the performance, we also witness the scattering of his ashes in the bay of Miyajima (Hiroshima). Part 4, 'The Mirror', tells the story of Jana Čapek, a Czechoslovakian-born Jew and Terezín survivor who also appears in the prologue as a student of Japanese martial arts. 'The Mirror' is structured as a mirror, with two paralleled settings: Hiroshima in 1986 and Terezín in 1943, with the latter being contained within the former. It also uses mirrors and mirroring techniques throughout. It shows Jana coming to Hiroshima to meet Ada, the surviving daughter of the Jewish opera singer Sarah Weber, who perished in the Nazi camps. As a child, Jana was detained at the Theresienstadt ghetto, established by the Nazis during the Second World War in the fortress town Terezín, where she befriends Ada's mother, Sarah Weber. When she learns of her imminent deportation, Sarah commits suicide, while Jana escapes thanks to a clever magician named Maurice. 'I believe Hiroshima chose me', Jana says in an interview in part 6.

'Ten years ago, I came to visit a friend and thought I would find devastation here, but instead I found beauty' (Lepage 1996: 106). Indeed, she found Czechoslovakia on visiting the Peace Memorial Park and discovering that the Atomic Bomb Dome in Hiroshima was built in Prague Secession-style. As Jana further explains, that kind of surprise is what initially attracted her to the silence of Buddhism. Indeed, as Robert Brustein notes about the play's 1996 performance at the Brooklyn Academy of Music, 'that kind of surprise – the reversal of normal expectations – becomes almost a structural principle of the play' (1997: 30).

Other strands of the play's plot include a traveling troupe of French-Canadian actors who come to Japan to perform a Feydeau farce at the Osaka world's fair in 1970 (part 5). The troupe's leading lady, Sophie, has a brief affair with a Canadian Embassy official, Walter Lapointe, only to be discovered by the diplomat's wife in a scene of adultery and exposure that mirrors the Feydeau plot. In part 7, the offspring of their sexual encounter, Pierre, comes to Hiroshima to study butoh dance and rents a room in Nozomi's house, which is now (in 1997) owned and occupied by Hanako Nishikawa, the widow of the Japanese Jeffrey (and Nozomi's daughter in the final version of the play). At the end of part 7 Hanako offers the familiar phoenix kimono that Nozomi wore when photographed by Luke to Pierre as a costume for his butoh dance. The gesture leads to a curious moment of transfiguration: as Jeffrey stretches his arms to let the kimono sleeves hang down, Hanako disappears behind it to be replaced by Jana. As Pierre then turns to face upstage, he too vanishes to reveal Sarah Weber slipping into the kimono. Commenting on this symbolic action, Scott T. Cummings writes in his review of the production: 'As much as the narrative itself, the play of images argues for reconciliation in interculturalism as the transcendant value to emerge from the end of "the American century." In this extraordinary creation, Robert Lepage and *Ex Machina* transform Hiroshima from ground zero into square one, a place where a new time of healing begins' (1997: 351).

As Fricker notes, critics largely 'embraced the production's ambitious sweep and humanist vision, and in particular highlighted its affectual power' (2020: 234). Robert Brustein called it a 'masterpiece' that 'explores America's responsibility for the horrors inflicted on Hiroshima in 1945', while attempting 'to show how suffering and sensitivity to suffering are human qualities that somehow manage to unite people' (1997: 29). Jim O'Quinn called it a 'masterwork of indirection – a monumental, impressionistic riff on the bombing of Japan, which the play likens to two other of the century's most formidable calamities', while Peter Brook described it as 'a theatre where the terrifying and incomprehensible reality of our time is inseparably linked to the insignificant details of our everyday lives – details that are so important to us, so insignificant to others' (qtd. in Fricker 2020: 233–4). For some critics, such as Jen Harvie, however, the fact that these 'personal and even domestic' fictional stories were set against the background of real-life, large-scale traumatic events was problematic in that the 'accumulation and mutual contextualisation' of Hiroshima, the Holocaust, and AIDS made 'them seem somewhat iconic, even generic' (qtd. in Fricker 2020: 234). I will address some of this criticism at greater length in the final part of my analysis of *The Seven Stream of the River Ota* here.

The new staging of *The Seven Streams of the River Ota* scheduled to go on a world tour in 2020 to mark the seventy-fifth anniversary of the bombings of Hiroshima and Nagasaki raises a number of thought-provoking questions. What do these first atomic bombings mean to us today, and what responsibilities do we have towards their victims? What did this act of historical violence reveal about the political moment? Can it be explained as a singular event in history? The atrocities in Hiroshima and Nagasaki were authorized and perpetrated in the name of rational judgement, with the use of the atomic bomb explained by many, then and now, as a necessary means of combating the evil of militaristic Imperial Japan: has the logic behind this justification of the decimation of entire cities been consigned to the pages of history? What is the symbolic value of those horrifying events today? Can we still write of the disposability of entire populations as a matter of urgency?

The atomic bombing of two Japanese cities by the United States that initiated the nuclear age was one of the worst things to have ever happened. In the case of Hiroshima (as so often is the way, Nagasaki is not actually mentioned in Lepage's performance), when the bomb with the explosive power equivalent to thirteen kilotons of TNT1 was dropped on a city of approximately 350,000 inhabitants, its blast instantaneously killed every human being within a one-kilometre radius. The abruptness and scale of the atomic attack on the civilians in Hiroshima left them utterly unable to comprehend what had happened. Those who survived the initial blast and its effects were exposed to piles of corpses and countless sufferers; as Robert Jay Lifton put it in his pioneering inquiry into the psychological impact of the atomic bombing in Hiroshima, they were literally 'immersed in death' (1967: 19–30). The bomb killed a multitude of children, women, and men living ordinary lives in an ordinary city in one stroke, and this cataclysmic and unprecedented event inaugurated a new, more precarious age in human history.

The bombing of Hiroshima was seen as having an inescapable eschatological dimension in its immediate aftermath; it was an event that had transformed everything and was seen to portend 'the spectacular intensity of a destructive end of the world' (Patočka 1996: 132). Despite the scale of the atrocity, however, its impact on social, philosophical, and cultural thought has not followed expectations. As the Czech philosopher Jan Patočka starkly states in reflecting on Hiroshima's historical legacy: 'Thus far the visible impact we could attribute to this fundamental transformation and conversion, not comparable with anything else ... has been nil' (1996: 132).

While, from a global perspective, Hiroshima has always remained somewhat foreign, removed, and even exotic, it has moved to the centre of the world's attention on those occasions when nuclear issues gained in urgency, in other words whenever the possibility of a future 'Hiroshima' rears its head. In his monograph *Hiroshima: The Origins of Global Memory Culture*, Ran Zwigenberg explores the development of memorialization – national and international – of Hiroshima's atomic bombing, comparing it with the memorialization of Auschwitz. He notes that pairing the Hiroshima and the Holocaust was commonplace before the 1980s, when the two discourses started to diverge (it is telling in this regard, as Zwigenberg observes, that the historian Eric Hobsbawm, who came of age in the first half of the century, uses the word 'holocaust' to refer to the 'nuclear holocaust'). Their separation can be partially explained by the fact that the atom bomb has not been used since those first two times in August 1945, while conflicts such as those in Bosnia and Herzegovina and Rwanda in the early 1990s, which included concentration camps set up to torture, rape, and kill thousands of unarmed civilians, including children, have given new fuel to the Holocaust discourse over the last seventy-five years. The fact that the Holocaust happened in the very heart of Europe is undoubtedly also significant to its continued visibility, with Hiroshima's non-Western, peripheral location likewise playing a role in its retreat from view. According to Zwigenberg, while the Holocaust and Hiroshima were initially treated as commensurable and part of the general challenge of modernity, our subsequent failure to maintain the connections between them 'obscures Hiroshima's importance for post-war global commemoration culture, including Holocaust commemoration, and its contribution to the development of the discourses of trauma, witnessing and progressive politics before the 1970s' (2014: 301).

In her book *Beclouded Visions*, Kyo Maclear explores the many myriad ways in which the atomic bombs dropped on Hiroshima and Nagasaki have shaped art, vision, and collective memory in the twentieth century. She argues that the trauma of Hiroshima and Nagasaki demonstrates the limits of dominant visual models, such as photography, in serving the needs of adequate historical memory. Drawing on a diverse array of images, including military photographs, Maclear asks what it means to see and witness such representations and asserts that putting a face to horror is not enough: 'To simply "picture" and "know" the human effects of the bombings has carried no assurance of ethical remembrance' (1998: 39). The US Atomic Bomb Casualty Commission (ABCC), for instance, which was founded under the directive of US President Harry Truman in March 1947 to examine the effects of radiation fallout on the bodies of the *hibakusha* (bombing survivors), turned them into objects of research rather than of treatment and responsibility. Human remains were taken from the debris of history to be tagged, charted, coded, and recirculated as silent documents. The evidence and photographs concerning the irradiated bombing victims, collected for purely clinical reasons, were not declassified for several decades. Furthermore, the Press Code imposed during the American occupation of Japan (until September 1951) applied also to all interpretative responses to the atomic bombings and censored anything written for broadcast or publication. Simply put, the US government did not want the evidence of bombings to circulate in order to quell dissent and garner support for future use of atomic bombs, a pressing possibility in light of the emerging Cold War era and Soviet nuclear capabilities. The public awareness of the *hibakusha* was even more limited and for much longer time outside of Japan, however.

When we look at the ABCC photographs today, it is clear that the photographed *hibakusha* seem thoroughly uncomfortable and conscious of their status as specimens. These photographs appropriated bodies from their social and historical biographies without acknowledging their victims' substantive and historical experiences. Those tasked with collecting the evidence, evoked in the character of the American army photographer Luke in the first part of *The Seven Streams of the River Ota*, were not there to empathize with or support the victims. The photos taken during the ABCC research mission did not address the specific historical character of their disfigurement but rather worked to freeze the understanding of the still-unfolding dimensions of *hibakusha* suffering. Through this mode of vision, 'suffering was depicted as *atomic*, that is discrete and manageable' (Maclear 1998: 39; her emphasis).

Photography in Lepage's performance, however, 'became a metaphor for seeing beyond immediate appearances to a deeper truth or understanding' (Fricker 2003: 91). This is apparent already in the first part of the play, which stages the encounter between Luke and the Japanese atom bomb survivor Nozomi. They become romantically involved after she asks him to take her picture because she has never seen her disfigured face. The scene effectively presents the absolute terror of the annihilating power of the atomic bomb without ever showing Nozomi's face, thus resisting victimizing her further by integrating her indescribable experience into a mechanical and rational intelligibility. During his second visit, Nozomi asks Luke if he would like a cigarette, to which he responds in the affirmative:

> *She holds a cigarette which he takes. He is still behind her. As he flicks his lighter open, she holds out her own cigarette. He then walks in front of her to light it, turning so he is facing the audience. He leans down to her. When he sees her face by the flame of his lighter, his expression turns to shock, and he stops moving. She takes his hand, and lights his cigarette with his lighter. Pause.*
> **Nozomi**   Surprising, isn't it?
> **Luke**   Yes it is... (*Pause*). (Lepage 1996: 6)

The irreducible gap between images and words, a gap that encapsulates the question of the visibility of the *hibakusha* or the visual possibility (of this scene), thus moves to the centre of Lepage's stage.

Lepage's dramaturgy here could be seen as consonant with Hans-Thies Lehmann's attempts to articulate a new politics appropriate to a postdramatic theatre that he offers in the epilogue of his influential book *Postdramatic Theatre* (German edition 1999; English edition 2006). Arguing that 'the mode of perception in the theatre cannot be separated from the existence of theatre in a world of media that massively shapes all perception', he draws connections between the search for ethical vision in theatre and visual cultures and practices proliferating in various arenas today that foster passive rather than engaged, even empathetic, looking. According to Lehmann,

> Theatre can respond to this only with a *politics of perception*, which could at the same time be called an *aesthetic of responsibility or (response-ability)* [...] it can move the *mutual implication of actors and spectators in the theatrical production of images* into the centre and thus make visible the broken thread between personal experience and perception. Such an experience would be not only aesthetic but therein at the same time ethico-political. (2006: 185–6; emphasis in the original)

In his view it would be absurd to see theatre as an effective alternative to the mass media spectacularization of political conflicts; instead, he is asking us to recognize the dialogic interactions between ethical engagement and spectacle embedded in visual acts of witnessing.

Lepage's *The Seven Streams of the River Ota* demonstrates that theatre can be a place for calling the lost and the dead – or recalling them – into the peculiar liveness of performance. In part 3 of the play, entitled 'A Wedding', Lepage invites us to remember the AIDS epidemic by depicting the assisted suicide of Jeffrey 1, an AIDS sufferer, in an Amsterdam clinic in 1985. The play thus recalls the 'plague years' of the crisis, namely the traumatic period between 1981, when the Centres for Disease Control and Prevention (CDC) in the United States first recorded cases of a rare strain of pneumonia among five white gay men, and 1996, when the advent of antiretroviral therapy reduced AIDS-related morbidity and mortality.

Historically, performance has proved to be a powerful means of intervening in the public understanding and experience of AIDS and of countering the subject's neglect by the cultural mainstream. As David Roman argues in *Acts of*

Intervention: Performance, Gay Culture, and AIDS (1998), AIDS performances in the United States in the 1980s and the 1990s did not just depict the social and historical context in which they were embedded; as forms of political intervention, they provided a different perspective on the events reported on by the dominant media, including those affecting gay culture. Many of those who saw the first production of *The Seven Streams of the River Ota* (1994–8), while the AIDS crisis was still ongoing, were very aware of, if not deeply affected by, the trauma and loss portrayed in part 3 of the play. Some people, including members of Lepage's cast, knew people who either died or were dying as a result of the epidemic. For others, the performance served as a jarring wake-up call to realities that mainstream culture would often rather ignore. Arguably, a quarter of a century later, the same may no longer hold for this play's spectators, for whom the relevance of these lessons to their contemporary times may well be unclear. As Fintan Walsh notes, 'Across queer communities in the West, incorporating the history of the AIDS crisis into successive generations' sense of the past has been a fraught affair, in part because of a desire to leave the past behind, made possible by changes in societal attitudes and law and advancements in antiretroviral treatment' (2019: 25). Indeed, there has been talk of the end of AIDS ever since the 1996 International AIDS Conference in Vancouver, where the success of protease inhibitors was officially announced, and especially in more recent years, given the development of preexposure prophylaxis (PrEP) medication that has already contributed to the dramatic drop in HIV acquisition in Western countries, such as the UK and the United States.

As Alisa Solomon argues, however, 'To talk about AIDS in the past tense, then, assumes a particular national and temporal framing, one that encompasses an all-consuming experience for a population whose survivors still feel its ravages' (2018: 5). The creative responses of HIV/AIDS activists to the death of tens of thousands of people, and to the rampant prejudice that made society slow to act on the growing evidence of an epidemic, have profoundly changed the cultural fabric of American society. Moreover, the AIDS crisis is far from over. The pandemic is still a global problem, with the United Nations (UN) counting nearly 37 million people as living with HIV worldwide (UNAIDS 2019). In the United States, where 1.1 million people are living with HIV, the disease disproportionately affects communities of colour (CDC 2019). In addition, only 40 per cent of people with HIV in the United States have access to necessary medications, with the current government reverting to the deadly indifference characteristic of the Reagan administration when the syndrome was first recognized (CDC 2019).

There has been a recent revival of performances that first emerged in response to the AIDS crisis in the United States, for instance of Larry Kramer's seminal play *The Normal Heart* (1985), which includes its 2014 HBO film version directed by Ryan Murphy. Like these revivals, in addressing the AIDS thematics, part 3 of Lepage's play has the potential to act as a catalyst for intergenerational exchange about not only the early years of the AIDS epidemic but also its effects on younger generations today. As one young gay activist from the United States testifies:

> The HIV/AIDS epidemic is alarming, with a disproportionate effect on the young, gay, poor and the communities of colour. Yet I still hope for a world with zero new HIV infections and zero deaths from AIDS ... A crucial part of achieving an AIDS free generation is recruiting a new contingent of HIV and AIDS activists to carry on the work my uncle began ... I want the next generation – including me – to step up and be counted to give millions of people affected by HIV and AIDS hope for a better world. (qtd. in Roman 2016: 127)

As this gay activist suggests, we are all haunted by the trauma of this both past and present disaster. In this respect, *The Seven Streams of the River Ota* is an important ethical project that renews, in its own way, the call to awaken us to this epidemic's continuing injustices.

Part 4, called 'The Mirror', features two paralleled settings: Hiroshima in 1986 and the concentration camp at Terezín in 1943. Jana Čapek, a Theresienstadt survivor, comes to Hiroshima to visit Ada, Jeffrey Yamashita's sister-in-law (a Dutch woman who married his half-brother). As we soon find out, Ada is the surviving daughter of Sarah Weber, a Jewish-German opera singer who befriended Jana in Theresienstadt. When Jana opens the doors of the wardrobe in the Hiroshima house, she finds herself facing two mirrors from which her memories of Theresienstadt start to emerge. During these mirror scenes (two to thirteen), Jana is seen as a child who meets Sarah Weber and is introduced by her to costumes (a yellow kimono), make-up, and Puccini's *Madama Butterfly*.

Located sixty kilometres northwest of Prague and halfway to Dresden, Theresienstadt (Terezín in Czech) had been an Austrian garrison town since the 1780s and a part of Czechoslovakia between the two world wars. It was annexed by Nazi Germany as part of Sudetenland in 1938, with the Theresienstadt ghetto formed there in November 1941 as a transit camp for Jews from the Protectorate of Bohemia and Moravia. For most inmates, Theresienstadt functioned as a holding space between their place of origin and their killing sites, with the majority eventually sent to their deaths. Altogether, more than 143,000 Jews were sent to Terezín, among them 74,000 Jews from the Protectorate of Bohemia and Moravia and 600 from the Sudeten area, 1,400 Slovak Jews, 57,000 German and Austrian Jews, as well as 4,900 from the Netherlands, 466 from Denmark, and 1,150 from Hungary. About 34,000 people died in Terezín, most of them elderly (Hájková 2020: 17).

With Czech, German, Austrian, Dutch, Slovak, and Hungarian Jews living side by side, Terezín constituted a significant site of transnational, albeit forced, encounters. Almost the entire Czech Jewish population had been sent to Terezín by the Nazis, with a smaller number of people sent there designated as 'meritorious' by the SS. While this group included a small number of artists – actors, scenographers, directors, musicians, and playwrights – Terezín was not a special destination for Jewish artists, with deportees coming from all segments of society. As Lisa Peschel writes in *Performing Captivity, Performing Escape* (2014), these artists would realize the survival strategies needed to make the intolerable situation at least comprehensible. Her critical collection, which features eleven theatrical texts written by Czech and Austrian Jews (including cabaret songs and sketches, historical and verse dramas, puppet plays, and a Purim play), reveals the broad range of ways in which prisoners relied on performance to engage with and escape from life in the ghetto.

A number of operas were presented at Terezín thanks to the conductors there. Raphael Schächter first put on Smetana's *Bartered Bride* and followed it later with Mozart's *Marriage of Figaro* and *The Magic Flute*, and Smetana's *Kiss*. Hanus Jochowitz, in turn, staged Mozart's *Bastien and Bastienne*, while Franz Eugen Klein conducted Verdi's *Rigoletto*, Puccini's *Tosca*, and Bizet's *Carmen*. Karel Berman directed Vilém Blodek's *In the Well*, and Viktor Ullmann put on *The Emperor of Atlantis*, which he wrote in Terezín (Hájková 2020: 35–6). A number of well-known female performers who survived the war were sent to Theresienstadt, among them Marion Podolier, Hedda Grabová, Josefa Klinkeová, Gertruda Borgerová, and Alice Herz-Sommer; it is not known, however, what they did and where they lived after the war, their traces having usually disappeared in its immediate aftermath. This could likewise be said of those who were murdered, for instance of Magda Spiegel, the alto operatic singer whose pre-war career was probably the most distinguished of all the musicians in the ghetto (she had been a prima donna in the Frankfurt opera) who was murdered in the Auschwitz concentration camp. While Spiegel continued to sing in the Theresienstadt and performed in the Requiem, her name comes up only on the margins of accounts about Terezín musical life, in contrast to those of Gideon Klein or Raphael Schächter. It was men rather than women who became Terezín's official chroniclers and canonized parts of its musical life. Among those often interviewed were Karel Berman, Karel Ančerl, Martin Roman, and Coco Schumann from the jazz band Ghettoswingers, with some of them also writing autobiographies.

The threat of deportation to the East was a daily reality for the prisoners throughout the camp's existence (1941–5), and one they saw as deadly. Transports left on a regular basis, at first for Riga and later for labour camps, ghettos, and annihilation camps in the Lublin district, Maly Trostinets, and Raasiku in Estonia, and, starting in October 1942, to Auschwitz-Birkenau (Hájková 2013: 509). From the more than 87,000 people who were sent from Terezín to the East, only about 4,000 survived (Hájková 2020: 12). This reality informs the end of the fourth act of *The Seven Streams of the River Ota*, when Sarah prepares to hang herself after learning of her imminent deportation from the ghetto by retelling the Butterfly story and donning her wig, make-up, and kimono. As Sherrill Grace writes of the play, 'the Butterfly narrative informs the diegesis, frames the action, and drives the plot, notably in its three most strategic parts – one, four, and seven' (2006: 147). While the basic narrative elements of Puccini's *Madama Butterfly* are present in part 1 (and thoroughly revisioned in part 7) of *The Seven Streams of the River Ota*, '[t]he only point at which *Madama Butterfly* is named and described is in part 4, and the only music from the opera to be sung – by a German Jew, not a Japanese Geisha – is that of the mother's farewell to her child as she begs: "guardo ben fiso, fiso di tua madre la facia che te'n resti una tracia"' (Grace 2006: 147).

Lepage takes a certain amount of poetic licence in his use of Puccini's *Madama Butterfly*, which was not performed in Terezín, yet the scene can be seen as a gesture of both incorporation and invention, an act of commemoration of a world believed by many to belong to another time and place. But, as Chambers points out, the scene also suggests that the full return of Holocaust survivors, such as Jana Čapek, would coincide with a new awareness on the part of the living of their own hauntedness, that is, of their connection not only to the survivors who haunt them but also to those who perished in the Holocaust and who haunt the survivors themselves (2004: 212). In a psychoanalytic sense, the scene functions as a work of mourning that strives to find form for grieving the great unmourned and bridging the living, the dead, and those yet to come. Even more fundamentally, however, the scene can be seen as invested in staging an imaginary encounter with the women who both survived and did not survive the Nazi genocide – through the testimony of the women themselves – thus not only increases our understanding of this terrible period in history but also makes us rethink our relationship to the gendered nature of knowledge itself.[1]

In regard to the question of whether it is appropriate to compare the various traumas that Lepage tackles in *The Seven Stream of the River Ota*, which made this performance so problematic for some critics, I want to recall here Cathy Caruth's meditation on communication across traumatic and cultural boundaries (already mentioned in this book's Section One) from the essay collection *Trauma: An Exploration in Memory* (1995) and her short monograph *Unclaimed Experience* (1996). Emphasizing the ethical value of bearing witness to trauma, Caruth argues that trauma can lay the ground for new forms of community by building bridges between disparate historical experiences:

> This speaking and this listening – speaking and listening *from the site of trauma* – does not rely, I would suggest, on what we simply know of each other, but on what we don't yet know of our traumatic pasts. In a catastrophic age, that is, trauma itself may provide the very link between cultures: not as a simple understanding of the pasts of others but rather, within the traumas of contemporary history, as our ability to listen through the departures we have all taken from ourselves. (1995: 1; her emphasis)

The appeal to a 'we' makes it clear that heeding the call to witness requires changing not only our notion of history but also our involvement in the histories of others.

Caruth elaborates on the ethical function of bearing witness to trauma in *Unclaimed Experience*, prompting us to rethink our engagement with otherness and to develop new and more just relations with others. In her chapter on Alain Resnais' film *Hiroshima Mon Amour* (1959), which some people found reductive for drawing parallels between mass catastrophe and historically less significant, individual loss, Caruth argues that 'in the case of traumatic experiences – experiences not of wholly possessed, fully grasped, or completely remembered events but, more complexly, of partially unassimilated or "missed" experiences – one cannot truly speak of comparison in any simple sense' (1996: 24). Following her line of thought, comparing experiences that consist of what has been missed in them – of what has, in fact, escaped our understanding – is not a comparison in its typical sense. As Caruth argues:

> Such a linking of experiences is not exactly an analogy or metaphor, which would suggest the identification or equation of experiences, since analogy and metaphor are traditionally understood in terms of what has been or can be phenomenally perceived or made available to cognition; the linking of traumas, or the possibility of communication or encounter through them, demands a different model or a different way of thinking that may not guarantee communication or acceptance but may also allow for an encounter that retains, or does not fully erase, difference. (1996: 124)

Since the publication of Caruth's *Unclaimed Experience* in 1996, the interdisciplinary field of memory studies has grown far beyond its nation-centred roots. Working against nationalism and ethnocentrism and 'building on the assumption that cultures and nations themselves are not static or clearly circumscribed but in constant active contact with one another', the field has arrived at a transnational and transcultural understanding of memory (Hirsch 2019: 11). This is reflected in the new terms used to qualify memory, for instance as 'cosmopolitan' (Levy and Sznaider 2006), 'multidirectional' (Rothberg 2009), 'transnational' (Erll and Rigney (2018), 'comparative' (Moses 2011), or 'connective' (Hirsch 2012). These crucial developments led to a transnational turn in memory studies that centres on questions of how memory is transferred and how it reflects cultural entanglements and interconnections. In this context, awareness of the possible dangers of comparison is a necessary counterbalance. Dirk Moses' warning about the potential of comparative memory, and especially the comparative memory of genocide, to relativize the violence perpetrated on specific populations, is warranted. Attentive to the ethical and political problems that attend the social flow of memory, Moses calls for an 'ethics of transculturality' (2014: 30) that would be sensitive to particularity and difference while also embracing those forms of solidarity that can emerge when diverse practices of remembrance are seen as implicated in one another. Within this framework, remembrance in *The Seven Streams of the River Ota* emerges as a mode of both thinking and doing – by bringing together bodies, relationships, and violent histories in unpredictable, new ways, it asks for their 'redress in relation to each other, rather than allowing them to stand separately and competitively as the exclusionary property of a single identity-based group' (Hirsch 2019: 12). As a result, the work remains 'sensitive to the limits of translatability among different contexts and histories, however entangled' (Hirsch 2019: 13). Rather than 'collapsing divergent experiences into false equivalences' (13), the performance foregrounds connectivity and entanglement while offering a distinctly transcultural approach to the intersecting memories of the represented remembering subjects, thus translating death, loss, and cultural amnesia into life-sustaining engagements with history and memory.

Even Pierre's butoh performance in part 7 can be seen as an act of solidarity and co-witnessing rather than of identification, or even of empathy with the victims of the atomic bomb. As Marianne Hirsch has noted in her seminal work on 'postmemory' (2012), cultural representations provide a powerful way of acknowledging traumatic legacies. The task of 'the generation of postmemory' is to claim these experiences and assimilate them into their own life story. As this book's Section One notes, Hirsch has expanded her discussion of postmemory to include what she describes as 'affiliative', rather than 'familial', postmemory, suggesting that postmemory is not 'limited to the intimate embodied space of the family' and may 'extend to more distant, adoptive witnesses or affiliative contemporaries' (2012: 6). Through Pierre's butoh dance, a dance form that emerged in response to the ravages of the Hiroshima and Nagasaki bombings, Lepage stages an encounter with the past that positions his body as a radically open meeting point between other bodies, voices, feelings, and histories. Thus framed, his body becomes both a material and a historical contact zone, an interface of cultural, affective, conscious, and unconscious transmissions.

SECTION THREE

Memory and Migration

The outbreak of the Arab Spring uprisings, the catastrophic war in Syria, and the rise of Islamic State triggered a crisis of enormous magnitude in the Mediterranean. 'The Mediterranean is today the centre of the world … [it] is the most problematic region in the world, and still the least integrated in the world', stated Federica Mogherini (2015), the High Representative of the European Union for Foreign Affairs and Security Policy. Mogherini spoke against the backdrop of a long and dramatic summer of 2015. The spectacle of humanitarian disaster was being broadcast through images of a Syrian toddler lying face down on the beach in the Turkish resort town of Bodrum; of rickety vessels overloaded with men, women, and children drifting in vast expanses of water; of mass arrivals on the shores of Greek islands; of families trying to make their way under barbed wire fences in the Balkans; and of the migrant crowds at Budapest Station. Together, they 'briefly brought into the light of day a long-repressed reality' (Kouvelakis 2018: 6). The spectacle was particularly extreme in two areas of the Mediterranean: the Aegean Sea and the waterway between Sicily and North Africa.

Typically described in public debate as the 'cradle of civilization' and a fertile space of mobility and exchange, this interface between Europe, Africa, and Asia has recently become a mass grave. From January to the end of August 2015, 300,000 refugees and migrants attempted the Mediterranean crossing, with approximately 200,000 of them landing in Greece and the rest in Italy (IOM 2017). Countless migrant boats went under in the Mediterranean waters. For people aiming to reach Europe, the Mediterranean Sea stands for the 'deadliest stretch of water' (UNHCR 2012). By the end of 2015, an estimated 3,800 died there, an increase of more than 15 per cent from the previous year. In 2016, following an accord between the EU and Turkey, the number of deaths rose considerably to exceed 5,000 for the first time – an increase of 35 per cent (IOM 2017).

As some critics have argued, the spatial politics behind this migratory situation makes the Mediterranean into 'a border zone of intertwining crises, i.e., the crisis of displaced populations, the crisis of the policies that govern mobility across European borders, and the Eurozone crisis with its effects on migration' (Garelli et al. 2018: 662). The discontinuity implied by such a crisis narrative 'conceals historical continuities, as well as the political process that has led to the contemporary situation' (Wolff and Hadj-Abdou 2018: 383). I have previously engaged with this crisis over a decade ago when writing about the human rights abuses in the Strait of Gibraltar and the dilemmas facing irregular migrants, refugees, and asylum seekers trying to enter 'Fortress Europe' (see Gluhovic 2008). Already two decades ago, Ahmed Ghazali, a Moroccan-Canadian playwright, addressed the material effects of the so-called non-arrival measures devised by northern countries to prevent irregular migrants from setting foot on their territories in his play *The Sheep and the Whale* (*Le mouton et la baleine*, 2001). The range of measures which were put in place more than a decade ago by the European Union (EU) member states, with deterrence being their key priority, have effectively undermined the right to seek asylum by blocking access to Europe. Their arsenal includes the imposition of visas for all refugee-producing countries, readmission agreements with neighbouring countries that form a 'buffer zone', immigration intelligence sharing and police co-operation, reinforced border controls, systematic detentions, and sanctions on carriers transporting migrants without the required travel documents and visas (Gluhovic 2008).

Practices of internment and detention in dealing with irregular migrants have grown more abundant in recent years. For instance, from 2000 to 2012, the number of detention camps in Europe has increased from 324 to 473, while increasing security concerns have at times compromised even the principle of *non-refoulement*, as Seyla Benhabib's recent and scathing critique of the EU's failure to live up to its own human rights commitments notes (2018: 122). This failure is manifest, moreover, in the removal of refugees from trains headed to Germany and writing numbers on theirs arms in ink by both the Czech and the Hungarian police; in the use of police dogs, tear gas, and water guns on protesting refugees by the Macedonians, the Slovenians, and the Hungarians; and in the inhumane living conditions and administrative procedures of harassment, incarceration, and deportation that irregular migrants are subjected to in open-air prisons, such as the Moria camp in Lesbos and the informal, now dismantled, camps of Calais referred to as 'the jungle' when in existence (2018: 101–2).

The plight of migrants today recalls Albert Cohen's reflection on what it means to be a refugee in the aftermath of the Second World War. During his address in Geneva in January 1949, at a meeting of the International Refugee Organization (IRO) and voluntary organizations, Cohen spoke of the three handicaps that he sees 'the refugee who is stateless' labouring under:

> The first lies in the fact that the refugee is an alien in any and every country to which he may go … He does not have that last resort which is always open to the 'normal alien' – return to his native country …

The second handicap lies in the fact that the refugee is not only an alien wherever he goes, but also he is an unprotected alien … He has no Government behind him … and the Bible says, 'Woe to the man that is alone'.

The third handicap lies in the fact that this man who is everywhere an alien, and an unprotected alien, is in the majority of cases an unfortunate, a piece of human flotsam … He is sometimes the object of the suspicion or contempt which are readily directed at aliens without protection; it is an accepted fact of mass psychology that the behaviour of a national group varies according to whether it has to deal with a 'normal' alien, reinforced with the invisible strength of the State whose protection he enjoys, or with the 'abnormal' alien, the refugee, powerless and unprotected, who in the last resort is unable to return to his native country – and who for that very reason, and most unjustly, is often treated as a suspect and an undesirable. (qtd. in Stone 2018: 104)

Cohen concluded his address with these words: 'It is obvious from all this that if there is any human being who needs protection it is the refugee' (qtd. in Stone 2018: 105). Seventy years later, Cohen's observation is no less obvious.

The processes of becoming a refuge, of migration, of admission to a new country, and of building a new life there, witnessed again today on a global scale, also resonate with Hannah Arendt's discussion of 'the right to have rights', a formulation that has both inspired and baffled theorists and lawyers ever since it was first made. Addressing the predicament of statelessness in Europe during the interwar period of 1918–39, Arendt points to the paradoxical nature of state sovereignty and its relation to belonging and rights:

Not the loss of specific rights, then, but the loss of a community willing and able to guarantee any rights whatsoever, has been the calamity that has befallen ever increasing numbers of people. Man, it turns out, can lose all so-called Rights of Man without losing his essential quality as Man, his human dignity. Only the loss of a polity itself expels him from humanity. (1973 [1951]: 297)

The problem stems from the stark dichotomy between human rights and citizens' rights. When massive populations in Europe became de facto stateless, they were left without recourse to the protective remedy of any legal regimes, since it is only by virtue of being part of a state, political community, or polity that one has rights. For Arendt, the paradox at the heart of human rights discourse is starkly embodied in the stateless person, who appears to be human and yet exists entirely without rights for the simple reason of not being attached to a state. The question this paradox gives rise to is troubling: do we have rights because we are human beings, or are we human because we have rights? The entire problem with human rights, in Arendt's view, is that they are invoked at the precise moment at which civil rights – one's rights as a citizen, the political artifice that bestows dignity – are stripped away. What follows is the sense of 'the abstract nakedness of being human and nothing but human' – a condition that Arendt sees as essentially 'worthless' (1968: 297) despite the best intentions of humanitarianism and its loquacious declarations of human rights.

The years following the Second World War saw an emergence of human right treaties, including the two most important international legal documents governing cross-border movement, namely the Universal Declaration of Human Rights (United Nations 1948) and the Geneva Convention of 1951 Relating to the Status of Refugees along with its 1967 Protocol. These and other human rights treaties have arguably allowed human rights to come of age by recognizing the rights of a 'person' independent of any legal state's regime, yet state consent remains at their basis. The Convention and its Protocol, for instance, are binding only for signatory states 'and can be brazenly disregarded by non-signatories and, at times, even by signatory states themselves' (Benhabib 2004: 11). The international human rights norms that emerged in mid-twentieth century did not solve the principal problem of the refugee as identified by Arendt – the problem of legal protections independent of citizenship or state consent.

Notwithstanding these two examples from recent historical memory, the public debate about refugees and border-crossing in Europe as well as in other parts of the world, for instance in Australia and at the US-Mexico border (Cox 2015; Dear 2015), often tends to be ahistorical. The situation is presented as a sudden, unpredictable emergency and depends on a selective memory of Europe's histories of emigration, refugee production and reception, and colonialism. As Kate Darian-Smith and Paula Hamilton argue in *Remembering Migration*, 'despite renewed interest from scholars in the historical dimensions of migration, there is a serious shortfall in the analysis of its remembrance' (2019: 2). Even the field of Holocaust studies, a key area of memory studies, is not immune to such omissions. As Debórah Dwork and Robert Van Pelt observe, 'Few histories of the Holocaust include discussions and analyses of the refugee experience' (2009: xii–xiii). This is astonishing given that more than half of the Jews of Germany, Austria, and Czechoslovakia managed to flee before the outbreak of the Second World War and that the Jewish refugee experience and response to them was truly global. As Tony Kushner rightly notes, the fact that 'there are few if any links made between the boat migrants of the twenty-first century and the "illegals" of the 1930s/40s reflects the self-contained nature of Holocaust studies (and, within it, Jewish refugee studies from that era) and the ahistorical nature of migration studies' (2017: 304). To Kushner, such 'exclusive readings of the past hinder the universalism proclaimed in the Charter of Lampedusa', which recognizes that 'The history of humanity is a history of migration' (2017: 304).

Warding off this universalism, Debarati Sanyal argues that thinking through continuities between contemporary traumatic journeys and those from the past when seeking to understand contemporary border practices may prove insufficient, since 'paradigms from the past may not be supple enough to account for their violence, nor for how such violence is negotiated, eluded, or resisted' (2017: 5). In contrast to those theorists of the refugee experience for whom the operations of contemporary borders materialize a state of exception that finds its historical emblem in the Nazi camp, such as Giorgio Agamben, Sanyal argues against reducing the heterogeneity of contemporary migrant camps to the singular paradigm of Auschwitz. She argues, instead, for envisioning the self-organized refuges, shantytowns, and other borderland encampments, as well as humanitarian camps and open-air detention sites, in all of their diversity, and for adapting our conceptual frames accordingly. Although the scenes of refugees bearing witness to their own dehumanization invoke disparate histories of racialized violence, they are irreducible to the experience of the Nazi past. And as Aimé Césaire, Frantz Fanon, and Arendt have argued, the Nazi camp itself 'is not a unique locus of biopolitics but requires historical rethinking in relation to sites such as the plantation and the colony' (Sanyal 2017: 13). In viewing the spectacle of unjust and failed responses to the migrant crisis, 'we' are inevitably implicated in the conditions of its making. As Ariella Azoulay has argued in *Civil Imagination*, 'the central right pertaining to the privileged segment of the population consists in the right to view disaster – to be its spectator' (2012: 1). We live in a radically unequal world. But what can be done with that knowledge?

In his book *The Beneficiary*, Bruce Robbins looks at the emergent recognition in the global North that the wealthy and relatively wealthy from the developed world owe their prosperity to the poor of the global South. He provides an important account of how a significant number of people who live in wealthier parts of the globe have come to be troubled by that inequality. Robbins identifies this growing discomfort with an incipient moral consciousness that can potentially be directed towards a politics of equality and the common good. As one of his examples, he uses a powerful passage from George Orwell's *The Road to Wigan Pier* (1937) to recuperate 'a creatively cosmopolitan voice grappling with the dilemmas of global economic justice' (2017: 9): 'Under the capitalist system, in order that England may live in comparative comfort, a hundred million Indians must live on the verge of starvation – an evil state of affairs, but you acquiesce in it every time you step into a taxi or eat a plate of strawberries and cream' (qtd. in Robbins 2017: 9). Orwell's notion of an everyday and largely unconscious acquiescence in an unjust system defines the life of the beneficiary that he (as well as Robbins) brings into a discomfiting light. For Robbins, recognition of this causal relationship distinguishes the discourse of the beneficiary from that of humanitarianism, which provides a very different epistemological frame for making sense of inequality. In humanitarianism, moral responsibility for distant others is premised on compassion for their suffering, but such compassion is not dependent on understanding one's implication in it. Orwell's primary contribution from Robbins' perspective is seeing that we are all connected by an exploitative system. 'The financiers and insurance company directors and bankers may run the system and profit egregiously from it', he writes, 'but in the global perspective, the global perspective that for Orwell trumps all others, we too, as taxi-taking and strawberry-eating inhabitants of the metropolis, are the system's beneficiaries' (2017: 36). The beneficiary class complicates simple class-based leftist politics in being, as it were, both the exploiter and the exploited. Robbins' book reveals some hidden possibilities and masked violences that can serve as levers in unsettling the commonsensical and allowing new possibilities into the world, yet it still leaves us grappling with how to confront the many unresolved injustices of our world.

Michael Rothberg's concept of the implicated subject, introduced in Section Two, seems to offer a greater and more heterogeneous analytical purchase than does the concept of the beneficiary as deployed by Robbins. Like beneficiaries, implicated subjects occupy positions aligned with power and privilege without being direct agents of harm themselves. Implication is not limited to economic injustice, deriving also from racism, colonization, and environmental catastrophe, among other social ills. Implicated subjects both benefit from and contribute to, inhabit and inherit, regimes of domination that they neither created nor control. There is a difference between feeling guilty for events that happened before we were born, which is neither necessary nor desirable, and taking responsibility for repairing some of these past wrongs, which is needed and commendable. As descendants of historical violence – from slavery to colonialism, genocide, and apartheid – we should do more than pay only lip service to the legacies of suffering and injustice.

In the context of the current discussion, this involves reflecting on the implication of European societies in the production of the migration crisis that is currently unfolding in various places across the globe. Of significance are issues of their military involvement in the Middle East, and economic exploitation, the 'neo-colonial' inequalities, and 'imperialist' domination that persist, for instance, in the EU-Africa relations. Similarly, Europe's inability to respond to wars, dictatorships, and disasters in sustainable ways warrants attention. The concept of implication, which articulates how legacies of past and present violence reside within us across space, time, and generations, can help to illuminate what is at stake here morally, ethically, and politically.

The field of theatre and performance studies has seen an uptick in research and creative responses as a result of the migrant crisis. This is clear from conferences like the 2018 International Federation for Theatre Research (IFTR) conference in Belgrade, as well as many important performances and publications created in recent times, including the *RIDE* special issue and monographs by Emma Cox, Alison Jeffers, Yana Meerzon, Silvija Jestrović, and most recently Steve Wilmer's *Performing Statelessness in Europe*. This book's focus on the nexus of memory, theatre, and performance calls for a consideration of what a specifically memory-inflected response to the migrant crisis might look like. The two performances that will serve as case studies here both look at how younger generations can best remember and move on from the past and what the activist legacy for the present should be, though they do so in different ways. The National Theatre production of *Small Island*, adapted by Helen Edmondson from Andrea Levy's prize-winning novel and André Amálio's performance *Portugal Is Not a Small Country* are the two recent theatre projects that will be discussed here in terms of their approaches to the subject of migration and memory. *Small Island* recovers and revisits the history of the Windrush generation in the UK, raising questions of how this history can be reclaimed in service of today's ongoing struggles against racism and inequality. *Portugal Is Not a Small Country*, in turn, revisits the contested terrain of Portugal's colonial history. As a European colonial power, Portugal has long existed within two zones, or time-spaces: within both a European and a colonial zone, and occupying a peripheral and backward position in both. As Boaventura de Sousa Santos (2009) has argued, for Portugal, as for its former colonies, lagging behind meant having a problematic past – and as a problem, the past became an inescapable part of the present.

Case Study 1: Andrea Levy's
Small Island

In his essay entitled 'Reconstruction Work: Images of Post-War Black Settlement', Stuart Hall comments on news agency photographs of the arrival of the Caribbean people taken at major London rail stations of Paddington, Victoria, and Waterloo. As they stood waiting to be met, or simply acknowledged, at these crowded stations, buttoned down against the freezing weather, these men, women, and children were '"dressed up to the nines", formally, for "travelling" and even more for "arrival"' (1991: 152). As Hall observes, their formal appearance counters expectations. 'Why does everybody wear a hat? Why are they carrying their clothes in straw baskets? Why do they look so respectable? Where are the street fighters, the rude boys, the rastas, the reggae?' (1991: 152). He explains it as follows:

> The people are 'dressed up' because they are on the longest one-way journey of their lives, literally and figuratively. Jamaicans travelled as they went to church, or visited their relatives – in their 'Sunday best'; the best thing you had in your wardrobe, for special occasions. The suits and dresses are the clothes of someone who is determined to make a mark, make a favourable impression. The formality is a signifier for self-respect. These are not the victims of migration, like the Jews and East Europeans photographed by Thomas Hine arriving at Ellis Island in New York. These folks are in good spirits. They mean to survive. The angle of the hats is universally jaunty, cocky. Already, there is *style*. 'Face the music, darling, and let's make a move.' (1991: 153).

One of the photographs Hall discusses here, included alongside a 1956 *Picture Post* article entitled 'Thirty Thousand Colour Problems', showed crowds of West Indians who had arrived by boat waiting at Customs. It constructed the arrival of black migrants from the Caribbean as a problem, with 30,000 of them expected in the UK that year. Each subsequent period has laid its own inflection on this image: for Hall, writing his essay in 1988, this archival photograph is interesting as it does not fit 'with either "Jamaica", the Black Nation, or "Jamaica", the sign of the Tropical-Exotic' (1991: 3). Drawing on Walter Benjamin's 'On the Concept of History', Hall reminds us that the sense of history emanating from this or any other archival image is never confined to the past. Rather, it requires 'a delicate excavation, an archaeology, a tracing of the contradictory imprints which previous discourses have stamped, through those old images, on the iconography of popular memory' (1991: 4).

In the aftermath of the Windrush scandal of 2018, when the British government sought to 'deport' its own citizens through a racialized process of stripping away their rights and citizenship entitlements, these lines resonate particularly strongly. It is this scandal that underpins Levy's *Small Island*. It started when it came to light that a generation of children who had arrived in the UK under their parents' passports were under threat of deportation for lacking citizenship documents, even though many had lived in the UK for upwards of fifty years. Amelia Gentleman's book *The Windrush Betrayal: Exposing the Hostile Environment* (2019) takes a closer look at what happened. Many of those affected had been born British subjects and arrived in the UK before 1971, particularly from Caribbean countries, as part of the 'Windrush generation'.[1] The term designates people who arrived in the UK from the Caribbean between 1948 and 1973 and comes from the name of the ship – *Empire Windrush* – that brought the first group of the Caribbean people to the UK in 1948, thus inaugurating the process of post-war mass migration from the region. Its import, however, resonates well beyond this now-legendary historical watershed.

So what does it mean to call forth this memory of the 'Windrush generation', as Levy does in her novel (and Edmundson in her stage adaptation of this material) – to have it flash up today, to paraphrase Benjamin – when contemporary politics in times of austerity disrupts the historical linkages between the imperial subjects of the past and their transformation, through decolonization, into today's 'immigrants'? What does it mean at the present juncture, when hard-right forces that have surged to power in this liberal democracy draw a sharp dividing line between the British Empire and its colonies, on the one hand, and the UK as a nation-state, on the other? Current British politics continue to uphold both the historical exclusion of immigrants (even those who were once citizens of the British Empire) and the image of British imperialism as a benevolent and progressive system. Finally, and crucially for this discussion, how does bringing the Windrush epic to the stage at the National Theatre in London in 2019 intervene in the UK's public sphere and resonate in the aftermath of the 2018 scandal?

What do we in fact remember on hearing 'Windrush'? In *Beyond Windrush: Rethinking Postwar Anglophone Caribbean Literature*, J. Dillon Brown and Leah Reade Rosenberg write:

In contemporary Britain, 'Windrush' stands metonymically as a marker for the emergence of an increasingly multicultural national polity, in which the old self-understanding of Englishness as racially white gradually cedes prominence to a newer conception of Britishness – one that strives to include the burgeoning population of citizens who trace their heritage back to the once-colonized spaces of the British Empire. (2015: 3)

The fiftieth anniversary of the inaugural *Empire Windrush* voyage in 1998 was marked by a number of explicitly memorializing acts, including the opening of Windrush Square in Brixton, the unveiling of a memorial stone and rose garden in West Green, and the introduction of an annual 'Windrush Sunday' to the national calendar. These gestures certainly mark the iteration of the Windrush as a cultural symbol (Mead 2009). The opening ceremony of the London 2012 Olympic Games featured an arrival of a newsprint collage ship standing in for *Empire Windrush*, which similarly 'communicated that post-war migrants from Britain's former colonies have become part of London's heritage' (Cox 2014: 58). However, for all the nostalgia that has subsequently come to be attached to this moment and the revisionist history that romanticizes the Windrush generation as a national treasure, it would be erroneous to construct this episode as the initiation of race in Britain. Treating the Windrush generation as the unquestionable origin of mass migration to the UK, as historians, journalists, literary critics, and cultural theorists currently tend to do, does not account for a history of complex migrations and mobilities in the aftermath of the Second World War.[2] The re-imagining of the Windrush across various cultural forms as 'a revolutionary rupture in a national identity imagined as homogeneous' (Mead 2009: 137) has effectively operated to divorce black presence in Britain from its broader project of colonialism and empire-building. The salient point that needs to be made in discussing Windrush is that it was a case of the empire coming home. The discrepancies between the cultural memory of the post-war immigration boom in Britain and the documentary evidence from historical records speak to a 'tension between memory as a safeguard against attempts to silence dissenting voices, and memory's own implication in that silencing' (Hodgkin and Radstone 2006: 16).

The failure to acknowledge the multicultural histories of colonialism and empire as integral to our understandings of the contemporary political situation is not unique to Britain. The association of multiculturalism with post-war migration to Europe has entrenched a very particular understanding of it within the European public sphere. Multiculturalism, and the presence of minorities more generally, is often presented in public discourse there as something that happened to Europe and against the wishes of wider European populations, possibly at the instigation of political elites. It is also frequently repudiated by the hard-right forces that have recently surged to power in liberal democracies across Europe (and indeed the globe). Campaign slogans of various European political parties and movements – for instance, 'France for the French' (Le Pen and the Front National), 'Take Back Control' (Brexit), 'Our Culture, Our Home, Our Germany' (Alternative for Germany), 'Pure Poland, White Poland' (Poland's Law and Justice Party), or 'Keep Sweden Swedish' (Sweden Democrats) – vividly illustrate this point. Across Europe and especially in Northern Europe and former communist states, questions of belonging are once again becoming increasingly pertinent to political debate. Significantly, 'right-wing populist leaders are being elected on platforms of ethno-economic nationalism, Christianity, and traditional family values, promising to protect their populace against invasions by other peoples, ideas, laws, cultures, and religions' (Brown 2019: 5).

These narratives fail to acknowledge that most European states were as much imperial as they were national states – and often prior to, or alongside, becoming the latter. The kingdoms of England and Scotland are a case in point. Both had acquired colonies prior to the Act of Union in 1707 and continued these colonial conquests after their union, meaning they were imperial states prior to and alongside the process of becoming a conjoined nation-state. As Gurminder Bhambra argues, there are many implications of not accounting for the long-standing histories of connections between populations, including the fact that many migrants came in fact as citizens, or at least as subjects, of their own broader polities, namely colonial empires. One of them is the misidentification of the emergence of the multicultural state as a post-1960s phenomenon rather than seeing its beginnings as the colonial project (2017). David Lammy MP makes a pertinent and poignant point when reflecting on the Windrush generation scandal: 'When my ancestors arrived in this country under the Nationality Act of 1948, they arrived as British citizens. They were British subjects not because they came to Britain, but because Britain came to them, took their ancestors across the Atlantic, colonised them, sold them into slavery, profited from their labour and made them British subjects' (2018).

The people who disembarked from the *Empire Windrush* in 1948 were brought to fill labour shortages after the Second World War, in which many of the arrivals and their relatives had served. They did not come as migrants but as British citizens, having this status enshrined that year by the British Nationality Act, which gave all Commonwealth citizens who had previously been subjects of the Empire the right to migrate to the UK and to all of the social, economic, and political rights of its citizens. The piece of legislation was passed with the double intention of warding off growing calls for colonial independence and of maintaining an imperial connection with dominions such as Canada, which had formulated their own national citizenships. Nonetheless, the act formalized the customary practice of the past, namely the free movement of British subjects throughout the empire's domain.

This is the historical backdrop of Helen Edmundson's stage adaptation of *Small Island*, Andrea Levy's celebrated novel, which premiered in 2019 at the National Theatre in London. The production put the spotlight on untold or overlooked aspects of the collective British history, such as previously marginalized black, working-class, migrant, and diaspora experiences. Furthermore, by showing the continuities between experiences of black and white men and women both before and after the war in the framework of Britain's long history of colonialism, the production intervened in the collective process of forgetting how the commonwealth's colonies have co-created today's Britain. In representing past failures, it affirms support for contemporary migrant communities that arrive expecting opportunity to first find injustice and ingratitude. Staged in the aftermath of the Windrush scandal, the production also confronted lasting truths in its depiction of the blind discrimination eroding the social fabric.

The National Theatre's staging of *Small Island* follows the lives of a handful of characters, starting with Hortense, a well-educated black Jamaican woman who longs for a new life beyond rural Jamaica and marries in order to emigrate to the UK in 1948. There is also her childhood friend Michael, who is enlisted for military service, and Gilbert, her husband, a black Jamaican man who served in the Royal Air Force (RAF) during the war before emigrating on the *Empire Windrush* in 1948 and dreams of becoming a lawyer. The group is completed by Queenie, a white British working-class woman who opens her home to a succession of servicemen and migrants in the absence of her conservative husband, Bernard, a white British middle-class man posted to India during the war and caught up in the Partition strife.

In her book *Empires without Imperialism*, Jeanne Morefield points out that discussing empires without mentioning imperialism has a long tradition in Anglo-American scholarship. Consequently, such narratives are 'rife with not merely claims about the good intentions of imperialists, but with stories that stress a profound lack of imperial intention on the part of states and individuals, as though somehow much of the world's population ended up under British control ... by accident' (2014: 24). As the recently published popular histories by commentators such as Niall Ferguson (2003) and Jeremy Paxman (2011) illustrate, discussions of empire often present it in a benign form – based on its *Pax Britannica* period, for instance, or in terms of its contributions to 'the modern world'. Apart from the exceptional work of scholars such as David Anderson (2005) and Caroline Elkins (2005), few British historians of the empire have addressed the violence through which it was constituted and maintained. Conventional histories elide the fact that the British Empire, which covered one-fifth of the habitable globe in the late nineteenth century and governed over one in every five people on the planet, was 'a consequence of military endeavour, of the dispossession of native inhabitants, of the appropriation of land, of the exploitation of resources, of the enslavement of Africans and Indians, of theft, genocide, colonialism and imperialism' (Bhambra 2017: 26).

Tracing the tangled history of Jamaica and Britain, Levy's novel presents a counter-history that resists a singular articulation of the migration and empire experience. Her narrative contests the dominant mode of looking at Windrush as a moment of rupture and reclaims a pre-history of discourses and events that informed and even shaped Windrush and post-Windrush encounters. These include the pre-war histories of Hortense's middle-class upbringing and education in Jamaica, her witnessing of an unfolding, intergenerational mixed-race love affair, and Queenie's childhood as the daughter of a Lincolnshire pig farmer, including her ambivalent memories of the 'chocolate coloured' African man at the Empire Exhibition in 1925. The stage adaptation of Levy's novel evokes wartime collaboration to represent the marginalized history of the Caribbean people before Windrush. *Small Island* foregrounds the experiences of black servicemen through the characters of Hortense's cousin (and Queenie's eventual lover) Michael and her husband Gilbert. While an RAF sergeant, Michael took part in raids over Germany before being shot down over France and invalided home. After training in the US state of Virginia, in turn, Gilbert is posted to Yorkshire to continue training as an RAF airman. For these two men, along with many other West Indians who joined the war effort in defence of the empire, Britain represented 'the Mother Country'. This idea had been drilled into them through the education system, the Civil Service, and other sources of imperial ideology. Bernard's story, in turn, tells the relatively forgotten story of the British troops on the Indian subcontinent, whose demobilization was delayed in the immediate aftermath of Second World War in order to maintain the empire; by bringing the Indian theatre of war into the picture, Levy also evokes the hidden history of over 2.5 million South Asian men who volunteered for military service to create 'the largest volunteer army in history' (Andermahr 2019: 559).

While both the play and the novel depict the wartime sacrifices of the Caribbean community, it is their thwarted dreams that prove the more inescapable theme. The Jamaican servicemen who were promised equality on signing up to the army are shown being greeted with suspicion and derision; the teaching qualifications that Hortense obtains in the commonwealth colony of Jamaica are deemed unsuitable for a job in England; even Queenie, who bravely defies the tides of racism dividing post-war society, is subject to trial by association. Overall, a community that served the empire and was promised an equal opportunity to live and work in Britain is shown in *Small Island* as being treated like second-class citizens.

It is a powerful depiction of the ways in which racism, operating on individual, social, and institutional levels, was experienced during the war by black military servicemen and in post-war British society by migrants in search of housing, employment, and parity in everyday encounters. The work shows how white people's attitudes to black people changed after the war from relative acceptance and tolerance to implicit or explicit hostility and resentment. Gilbert, for instance, experiences institutional racism during training and employment in both the armed forces and civilian life. Instead of realizing the dream of becoming a pilot, Gilbert is assigned a ground staff role like the majority of other black servicemen. In Gilbert's case and to his great disappointment, he is sent to the transport division to become a driver. When he returns to the UK as a migrant on the *Empire Windrush*, in turn, he intends to study law but is only able to get trades-related training in bread-baking, which he rejects out of pride. He also encounters racism on the job market, facing rejection from even menial jobs on the grounds of his race. When he eventually gets a job with the Post Office, Gilbert is constantly subjected to racist bullying and aggression. During one such attack, he is asked: 'When are you going back to the jungle?… Oi, darkie? You ain't answered me. When are you going back where you belong?' (Levy 2019: 95). Levy's novel also depicts Gilbert's experience of racism in his search for housing as he is repeatedly turned away from rental properties. As Gilbert wryly sums it up:

> Man, there was a list of people who would not like it if I came to live – husband, wife, women in the house, neighbours, and hear this, they tell me even little children would be outraged if a coloured man came among them. Maybe I should start an expedition – let me trace it back and find the source of this colour bar. (Levy 2004: 215).

Sonya Andermahr argues that 'Gilbert's comment "let me trace it back"' shows his (and Levy's) understanding that white/black relations are not just a consequence of war but are shaped by the long history of slavery and colonialism' (2019: 561). When Gilbert finally rents a room at Queenie's house, he must again weather the racist attacks of her husband Bernard. His response to Bernard is telling:

> Your white skin. You think it gave you the right to lord it over a black man. But you know what it make you? White.

That is all, man. White. No better, no worse than me. We both just finish fighting a war for a better world we want to see. But still, after all we suffer together, you wan' tell me that I am worthless and you are not. Am I to be the servant and you the master for all time? Because you are white? No. Stop this, man. We can work together, Mr Bligh. We want the same thing – a decent home, some work, some self-respect, some love. We can work together. You no see? Man, we must. Or we just go on fighting each other to the end. Fighting and fighting. And what then? What then? (Levy 2019: 127)

This play may respond to a particular time in history, but it also confronts lasting truths in its depictions of blind discrimination eroding the fabric of a society. What Stuart Hall wrote when reflecting on the *Picture Post* of 1954 also holds true for situations depicted in Levy's novel: 'English racism is not so much a single discourse as the interdiscursive space when several discourse are articulated together: the discourse of race, and colour, and sexuality, and patriarchy, and "Englishness" itself' (1991: 163). The play also shows the ways this situation is potentially traumatizing. Trauma studies scholars such as Stef Craps have made a compelling case for the need to expand the current event-based model to 'alternative conceptualization of trauma' as proposed by postcolonial critiques, such as 'insidious trauma', 'continuous traumatic stress', 'cumulative trauma', or 'oppression-based trauma' (2013: 4). Drawing on work critical of the American Psychological Association's model of post-traumatic stress disorder (PTSD), which informs much trauma theory, Craps calls into question the conventional definition of trauma as an event that 'would evoke significant symptoms of distress in most people' and that is 'generally outside the range of usual human experience' (2013: 24), such as military combat, rape, and torture. As Laura Brown points out, this definition ignores 'the normative, quotidian aspects of trauma in the lives of many oppressed and disempowered persons' (2008: 18), such as those of black people in racist societies. As the Black Lives Matter movement and the recent Windrush scandal starkly remind us, quotidian aspects of trauma are a constant presence in black people's lives; they constitute what Brown calls a 'continuing background noise rather than an unusual event' (1995: 103). At the same time, it must be remembered that racism against black people in the Western world, and particularly in the United States, still takes the form of overwhelming violence at times, as happened for instance with the murders in Charleston, South Carolina, in 2015.

Stories of black women and men who have lived in Britain for more than fifty years being sent back to the Caribbean in retirement expose the full reach of the normalized and entrenched racist politics and a broken system. While the current assault on the Windrush generation is a depressing expression of today's Britain, it also operates in dialogue with racism that seems to be more legitimately sanctioned against those named in public discourse as 'illegal immigrants', 'foreign criminals', and 'terrorism suspects'. In this respect, the denial, refusal, and withdrawal of citizenship exposed in the treatment of the Windrush generation also reflects the intensified deportation regime developed in the context of the ongoing war on terror, which has cultivated the most drastic legislative measures for citizenship deprivation in British history while developing a sophisticated infrastructure for mass deportation (Kapoor 2018). British citizens who are not recognized as such are now joining immigrants and asylum seekers in Yarlswood and multiple other detention centres around the country, where the outcast and most marginalized are criminalized for merely existing. Despite the Windrush scandal and subsequent public backlash, in February 2019, a charter flight with an estimated fifty people on board flew to Jamaica in the first known deportation since March 2017. The deportations of Windrush migrants and their descendants that took place under the aegis of Theresa May's hostile environment immigration policy should be seen in light of long-term state definition of who is deserving of care. They represent a longer history of welfare allocation based in shifting relations between race, ethnicity, and citizenship. As Lara Choksey writes, 'The issue is not these people's joblessness, health problems, or criminal behaviour: it is the final abdication of state responsibility for their welfare' (2019: n.p.).

This diffuse violence that hides behind rational categories of crime, poverty, and pathology continues to characterize black life in Britain today, obscured in its everydayness. The oscillation between the journeys from Jamaica to Britain in 1948, when *Empire Windrush* first docked at Tilbury, and the forced deportations from Britain to Jamaica in 2018 distil the past seventy years into one definitive moment. It confirms the ongoing impact of an already historical injury. Given this knowledge, is it enough that *Small Island*'s act of commemoration counters the disavowals constitutive of the British national community? Can this performance of collective memory of past transgressions ensure the end of injustice? Is remembering the only conceivable, or viable, form of political agency? Along with Saidiya Hartman in 'The Time of Slavery', I wonder: 'need we rely on the past in transforming the present, or, as Marx warned, can we only draw our poetry from the future and not the past?' (2002: 773).

In his seminal book *Performing History*, Freddie Rokem suggests that performance could

> create restorative energies, in the sense of recreating something which has been irretrievably lost and attempting, at least on the imaginative level and in many cases also on the intellectual and emotional levels, to restore that loss. These creative attempts aim at overcoming ... destructive energies without necessarily becoming a direct process of mourning for that loss. (2000: 13)

Rokem's vision of engaging with the past through performance in the present to rouse restorative energies to counterbalance a given loss seems apt given the aggravated nationalism and xenophobia confronting so much of the world today (Reinelt forthcoming). While the emphasis on remembering and working through the past in *Small Island* exposes our insatiable desires for curatives and healing, its injunction to remember becomes even more urgent in light of the contemporary migration narratives engaged with here, which elide the historical connections between today's national state and Britain's former imperial colonies to maintain a distinction between them and, by extension, between citizens and immigrants. This thematics is also at the centre of André Amálio's performance *Portugal Is Not a Small Country*, which deals with the Portuguese history of colonialism and now moves to the foreground of analysis. Amálio's performance demonstrates the need to narrate the European colonial past and see the implications of this past in the very project of Europe itself – with all the rights, duties, and obligations that reparatory justice entails.

Case Study 2: André Amálio's *Portugal Is Not a Small Country*

Between 2015 and 2017, André Amálio and the Hotel Europa theatre company produced a trilogy of performances about the end of the Portuguese empire in Africa. The trilogy comprises of *Portugal Is Not a Small Country* (*Portugal não é um País Pequeno*, 2015), *Pass-Port* (*Passa-Porte* 2017), and *Liberation* (*Libertação* 2017). Each performance combines written and audiovisual archive materials about one of three key periods in Portuguese history, along with testimonies collected by Amálio from people who lived through these times. In *Portugal Is Not a Small Country*, the subject is colonization and the discourses that anachronistically prolonged it; *Pass-Port* looks at the identity reconfigurations among people who came to Portugal from the former colonies between 1974 and 1976; while *Liberation* stages the independence struggles of former Portuguese colonies. The testimonies featured in *Portugal Is*

Not a Small Country come from ex-Portuguese settlers who were part of the refugee exodus from Africa between 1974 and 1976. *Pass-Port*, which was co-produced with Teatro Maria Matos in Lisbon (as was *Liberation*), investigates the impact of independence movements in former Portuguese colonies on Portuguese nationals, both those forced to move to Portugal to escape the revolutionary processes and the civil war and those who stayed in the newly independent countries. The last part of the trilogy, *Liberation*, draws on the testimonies of former soldiers and civilians who joined the independence efforts in the colonies, including archived political speeches of figures such as Agostinho Neto, António Oliveira Salazar, Amílcar Cabral, Eduardo Mondelane, Holden Roberto, Jonas Savimbi, Marcello Caetano, and Samora Machel, in order to tell a story of the wars of independence in Africa. In dissecting these historical events from the perspective of African freedom fighters and in light of their actions in Angola, Guinea-Bissau, and Mozambique, *Liberation* also reflects on these wars' impact on the Portuguese fascist regime – 'New State' (*Estado Novo*) – that eventually brought down the 'National Dictatorship' (*Ditadura Nacional*). Drawing also on the historiography of the Portuguese colonialism, as well as memory studies, political science, and philosophy, the trilogy reflects critically on a momentous era in Portuguese history, which all too often has been forgotten or wrongly figured as distant.

'There is a way of remembering things. There is way of remembering things collectively ...' So begins *Portugal Is Not a Small Country*, which tells a series of stories of *retornados*, or Portuguese 'decolonization migrants' (Smith 2003: 11), namely those who returned to Portugal following the 1974 Revolution and the onset of instabilities in the newly independent African countries. Some had been born in Africa, in fact, and had never been to Portugal before, although the majority were first-generation settlers in the colonies. Approximately 600,000 people, or about 6.5 per cent of the Portuguese population at that time, arrived from the ex-colonies, and particularly from Angola and Mozambique, making for the 'largest population movement in the history of 20th-century Portugal' (Lubkemann 2003: 76).

The process of 'decolonization migration' and its impact on Portuguese society have been largely silenced in the Portuguese public sphere, including academia, over the last few decades. The recent historiographic interest in the *retornados* views the question of decolonization largely in relation to the experiences of Portuguese nationals living in colonial metropolitan centres (see Ribeiro de Menezes 2016). The various social trajectories explored in *Portugal Is Not a Small Country* speak to over two decades of the *retornados*' experience in the aftermath of the 1975–6 migration wave, but the performance does not evoke other migrations and displacement that are possibly more pressing to commemorate and work through, be it the legacy of slavery and the history of displacements and dislocations from homelands in Africa, both during colonial times and in the aftermath of the independence wars. Amálio addresses these themes and issues in the rest of the trilogy.

Portugal Is Not a Small Country starts with Amálio entering a performance space that resembles an improvised kitchen and dining room, featuring two chairs, a small table, a black-and-white television, and a small electric cooking plate. He addresses the audience directly, explaining that the performance was devised from twenty-three interviews with former Portuguese settlers who had lived in Africa during the colonial period, whose real-life stories will be heard whenever the performer uses headphones. The first scene ends with an enactment of an interview with a *retornada* who left Portugal as a young woman to settle in Angola; it is her aeroplane journey back to Lisbon, already as a married woman with two children, that closes the performance.

Amálio presents the verbatim material as a collage made of diverse stories about leaving Portugal for the colonies, the settlers' lives in Africa, colonial and race relations, the start of the colonial/independence movements and wars, resistance to fascism, the role of women in Africa, the Carnation

Revolution and 25 April 1974, Lusotropicalism, international pressure on Portugal, and the settlers' return there. To shape this multifaceted, complicated history into a comprehensible narrative that is affectively present, Amálio inflects these stories with the different voiceprints of the interviewees, helping spectators link different people to specific topics.

As Sandra Richards notes, 'like theatre, memory is constructed through processes of selecting, repeating, forgetting – wilfully as well as unconsciously – and re-assembling narratives' (2005: 617). While its subject is in the past, memory often serves a presentist agenda. In other words, in reflecting on the past, 'our selection of facts, the emphases we devote, and the meanings we make are determined by our location in the present' (Richards 2005: 617). Supposedly, we often remember to learn from the past so that its lessons can illuminate our present and future, though this only contributes to a sense of irony when watching this performance, for the vast majority of the *retornados*' testimonies are imbued with Lusotropicalism and colonial nostalgia, featuring scenes of colonial paradise with stories of hunting wild animals, parties, eating shrimps, wealth, and freedom from their homeland's conservative norms. Amálio undercuts these nostalgic accounts by juxtaposing them with a critical commentary, autobiographical reflections, and archival sources (from the archives of Portuguese National Television, RTP). Among the latter is a 1930s propaganda video of Portuguese fascism rally at a stadium, a video of black native Africans dressed in traditional costumes dancing a Portuguese folk dance, footage from Marcello Caetano's official visit to London, and footage of the air rescue of *retornados* fleeing Angola in 1975.

The ideology of Lusotropicalism is evoked already in the title and poster image of the performance, namely a propaganda poster from 1934 displaying a map and the title *Portugal não é um país pequeno*. For the New State, the map was meant to show Portugal's greatness and emphasize the 'size' of the country when mainland Portugal and its colonies were taken as one (Amálio 2018: 70). Under the leadership of Salazar and

Caetano (1932–74), as Ricardo E. Ovalle-Bahamón (2002) notes, the Portuguese government actively advertised to the world and to itself a vision of Portugal without colonies. While the Portuguese presence in Africa and Asia was openly criticized in the new United Nations after the Second World War, in particular by the independence movements in Asia, the Salazar-Caetano regime firmly defended its position that Portugal no longer possessed colonies due to its ability to civilize and assimilate their indigenous populations. The New State devoted a great deal of effort and resources promoting Portugal as one across the continents, with residents of all territories controlled by the Portuguese State belonging to one great, multicontinental, and multiracial nation (albeit with varying political rights). A 1935 newspaper editorial from *The Portuguese World* (*O mundo Português*) says it all: 'we must always keep alive in the Portuguese people the dream of *além-mar* ("beyond-the-seas") and the pride and consciousness of the Empire.... Africa is for us a moral justification and a reason for being a power. Without it we would be a small country, but with it we are a great nation' (cited in Bender 2004: 6). Anecdotally, Amálio reports witnessing two men passing by the performance poster on the street and one of them remarking, 'You see and they still say that Portugal is a small country. Look at this!' (2018: 70). While this could have just plain ignorance, it could also signify that Lusotropicalist ideology and uncritical views of Portugal's history still persist in the present.

In his book *The Civilising Mission of Portuguese Colonialism, 1870–1930* (2015), Miguel Bandeira Jerónimo offers a critical historical analysis of the formation and development of the 'civilizing mission' doctrine of Portuguese colonialism between 1870 and 1930, paying particular attention to the question of native labour. Drawing on numerous archives and Portuguese, English, and French sources, he demonstrates that all the European empires had similar 'civilizing missions' in Africa and that the Portuguese, far from being an exception, were but one such power. While Portugal formally abolished slavery in its African colonies in 1878, Jerónimo shows that the legal end to slavery did not lead to a system of free wage labour in the Portuguese Colonial Empire. His analysis of policies adopted for the recruitment, employment, organization, and distribution of native labour in the Empire shows compulsory native labour to be a pivotal feature of the Portuguese colonial system in Africa. Under a thick veneer of progressive legislation prohibiting slavery, forced labour, and the ill-treatment of their African population, the Portuguese sugar-coated the brutal reality of their proficient extraction of forced labour from Africans who lived on the lands taken over by settlers. Jerónimo makes a convincing and exhaustive argument as to the central role of forced labour in Africa by highlighting the contrast between the idealistic legislative rhetoric and the reality of Portuguese colonialism. He shows that the labour system was supported and nurtured by old and resilient racial outlooks, which favoured multiple modalities of coercion and compulsion that substituted for slavery from legal and practical perspective. Labour, forced if necessary, was promoted as the foremost instrument in raising the native population to accepted civilizational standards. Behind the rhetoric of Portugal's 'civilizing mission', there lay a labour system centred on the brutal exploitation of native workers for the economic interests of private companies and the colonial administration.

The fundamentals of the 'new slavery' characteristic of the Portuguese empire between the nineteenth and twentieth centuries are grasped particularly well by Henry Rowley in his study *Africa Unveiled* (1876):

> the instructions which these governors [of African territories under Portuguese administration], major and minor, received from the home government are admirable. The blessings of civilization and Christianity are set forth in eloquent phraseology, and the duty of extending such blessings urgently enforced... Theoretically, nothing can be better than the position, the policy, and the character of the

Portuguese in Africa ... Practically, nothing can be worse or more humiliating. (cited in Jerónimo 2015: 1)

As Jerónimo amply demonstrates, Lusotropicalism in practice was never more than empty rhetoric justifying Portuguese colonialism in Africa and Asia on an ideological basis. The anticolonial movements, particularly in Africa, followed by the attainment of independence of the African colonies in the 1970s, challenged these assumptions and highlighted the need to re-think Portuguese history. It was also at this time that around 800,000 people relocated from the former colonies to Portugal.

Amálio challenges the hypothesis that Portuguese imperialism had a special, or exceptional, nature throughout *Portugal Is Not a Small Country*. The performance links the fundamental dynamics of Portuguese imperialism to those of other European metropoles, since it too was driven by global factors behind capitalist economic expansion, namely the search for new markets and natural resources (see also Morier-Genoud and Cahen 2012). To this end, the performance features the song 'Conqueror' ('Conquistador') by the Portuguese pop music band Da Vinci. As the 1989 winner of the Festival RTP da Canção, the song went on to represent Portugal at the Eurovision Song Contest and tellingly celebrates the then approaching 500th anniversary of Age of Discovery and the start of the Portuguese colonial empire. In *Portugal Is Not a Small Country*, Pedro Salvador and André Amálio perform 'Conqueror' in a way that challenges the celebratory perspective of its lyrics:

It was a new world
A dream of the poets
Go to the very end
Sing new victories
And proudly they raised flags
Living adventures of battles
that were a thousand epics

lives so full
They were oceans of love
I've been to Brazil Praia and Bissau
Angola Mozambique Goa and Macau
Oh, I went to Timor I have been a conqueror
It was an entire people
Guided through the skies
It spreads across the world
Following its heroes
And they carried the light of culture
With tenderness
Thousand epics
So full lives
They were oceans of love.
(cited in Amálio 2018: 225–8)

While it is sung, the song is interrupted several times by Amálio's autobiographical stories that engage with Portugal's difficult past. The aim is to prompt the audience to look critically at the song's lyrics and symbolism instead of adopting its celebratory point of view, and this to question the Lusotropicalism that is still felt across Portuguese culture and society.

It is at this point in the performance that Amálio also acknowledges his familial implication in the history of Portuguese colonialism. To frequent questions about his reasons for doing the show, which often presume a familial link to Africa, he replies:

No, no. I wasn't born in Africa, but curiously my parents lived in Africa. My mother lived in Lourenço Marques, now called Maputo, she was a nun there and lived there for some time. And my father also lived in Mozambique in Quelimane, he was a police officer there and was also there for a few years. And there's something here in this colonial heritage of my parents, which brings to mind the civilising mission of the Portuguese that António Oliveira Salazar spoke about, with my dad enforcing the law of the Estado Novo dictatorship and my mother preaching religion to small children. And that's why I'm doing this performance. (Amálio 2018: 229)

As his performance shows, the third Portuguese Empire was not the work of only heroes and satraps, be they politicians, bishops, military men, or rich businessmen. Most white settlers were poor, with emigration their only way to leave the Portuguese countryside for the city, even if they were in Africa (which, as the state claimed, was part of Portugal itself). While historiography has underestimated and understudied these communities, some of the recent scholarship shows Portugal's heavy reliance on diasporic/emigrant groups in the creation and sustenance of its empire (see Morier-Genoud and Cahen 2012).

The *retornados* who arrived in Portugal as the former colonies gained their independence became signifiers of colonialism in the country. Their presence inspired a transformation of the Portuguese nation. It also prompted the re-invention of Portugal and the Portuguese people as part of the European nation-state system, which meant distancing the nation from colonialism and simultaneously alienating the *retornados* from Portuguese nation-ness. In Portugal, decolonization led to the reconstruction of colonialism as limited to the presence and actions of those living in the colonies rather than a complex and entrenched system of political and economic structures (Ovalle-Bahamón 2003). *Retornados* were represented as a 'foreign' element embodying a past age of colonial exploitation that had been denounced in both global and local discourse.

By way of conclusion, a look at the ways in which *Portugal Is Not a Small Country* points to some limitations in how the Portuguese empire is recalled. As Paulo de Medeiros has commented, in Portugal there is still

a certain hesitation in studying questions of individual and collective trauma with regard to the political history of the country, and the form in which this latter has conditioned not only individual daily life but also the construction of national identity. In a country where History and historiography play a determining role, it is curious to find so little attention paid to studies of cultural memory that take a critical stance, rather than those that simply identify and extol the supposed central categories of an identity that is assumed to be homogenous. (qtd. in Ribeiro de Menezes 2016: 87)

In other words, Portugal has much memory work to do as regards her 500 years of colonial history.

In his doctoral dissertation, Amálio identifies, via reference to Ricoeur, the main ethical impetus behind his project as the duty of memory: 'the duty to do justice, through memories, to an other than the self' (2004: 89). He also writes: 'I believe that my duty to this work is to do justice to the colonised, the people that have suffered under the oppression of colonialism and for those who suffer from lusotropicalism today' (2018: 74). He confesses: '[it has] helped me to think that I was not speaking for the retornados and not even speaking about the retornados, but about a period of Portuguese history that they witnessed, a history that has been silenced and that I wanted to understand' (2018: 74). In this effort, Amálio is joined by an increasing number of artists producing work that responds to this past. Among them are some theatre artists who lived through that period, such as Angela Ferreira, Manuel Botelho, Isabela Figueiredo, and Dulce Maria Cardoso, while others represent younger (post-memorial) generations (namely, Filipa César, Mónica Miranda, Grada Kilomba, Joana Craveiro, and Jorge Andrade, among others). Many of these artists explore the Portuguese colonial past by deploying methods similar to Amálio's: engaging colonial archives, gathering oral testimonies, and utilizing autobiographical materials. Recent years have also seen a rise in the initiatives of black activists, among them: Djass, an association of African descendants founded in 2016; Consciência Negra (Black Conscience), a political organization founded in 2015 and engaged in the fight for black rights; SOS

Racismo, an anti-racist association founded in 1991; *Afrolis*, an audioblog about black issues started in 2014; Lisboa Africana, an association founded in 2012 and focused on promoting African events in Lisbon; and Plataforma Gueto, an anti-racist group founded in 2012. One recent accomplishment of the black Portuguese movement came in 2017 with the approval for a monument commemorating victims of slavery to be built in Lisbon. As the first of its kind, the monument was proposed by Djass and chosen by popular vote, a sign that the move to fight for structural decolonization today is achieving important visibility and support in Portuguese society today (Amálio 2018: 30–1).

Theatre and Memory in the Age of the Anthropocene

At the beginning of this chapter, I addressed the European refugee crisis, especially in the heavily policed Mediterranean space, asking what can be done in order to reclaim the material, social, and legal conditions for the acceptance of refugees in Europe and to establish unity, solidarity, and hospitality in Europe against a transnational front of the forces rejecting refugees. At the same time, I remain aware that, as my colleagues Emma Cox and Caroline Wake have argued, the hypervisibility of the European refugee crisis can occlude other crises elsewhere in the world in Africa, Southeast Asia, Australia, and the Asia Pacific region (2018: 140). Indeed, in the past fifteen years, we have witnessed suffering masses of refugees, asylees, and internally displaced persons from the Global South and East desperately trying to reach the resource-rich countries of Europe as well as Canada, the United States, and Australia, with the conditions of refugees reaching crisis proportions not encountered since the Second World War. As a report by the United Nations High Commissioner for Refugees shows, 65.6 million people were displaced by conflict, violence, or economic and ecological disasters by the end of 2016 (UNHCR 2017).

Saskia Sassen usefully reminds us in *Expulsions: Brutality and Complexity in the Global Economy* that the global refugee crisis is but one in a larger system of expulsions that characterize contemporary capitalism. Sassen argues that this massive and diverse set of expulsions – from professional livelihood, from living space, and even from the very biosphere that makes life possible – is actually signalling a deeper systemic transformation that is taking us into a new phase of global capitalism and global destruction. The expulsions Sassen analyses cut across domains conventionally imagined in separation, from financial rationality to poverty, and from displacement to environmental problems. The connections the migration crisis is making apparent are caused by what the author calls 'predatory "formations," a mix of elites and systemic capacities with finance a key enabler, that push toward acute concentration' (2016: 13). The three forms of expulsions at the core of the book are: a steep rise of poverty rates, growing forced displacement, and massive expansion of the penal state. Arguing that parts of our economies, societies, and states in Europe are being stripped bare by an extreme form of predatory capitalism, the author notes that, in 2012, '24.2 percent of European citizens were at risk of poverty, severely deprived or living in households with very low work intensity' (2016: 51). Next, 2011 was 'the fifth year when the number of forcibly displaced persons worldwide exceeded 42 million' (2016: 55), while in 2011 the Global South hosted 80 per cent of the world's refugees. Finally, she registers the massive expansion of penal apparatuses across the global North and South, noting that at present one in thirty-one US citizens is detained, on probation, or on parole (2016: 65). Sassen draws surprising connections to illuminate an unprecedented severe exacerbation of these expulsions. It is unprecedented not only because of its geographical breadth but also because it cuts across apparently disconnected and different social, economic, and environmental issues. In all these cases, the myriad 'expulsions' of people, places, and nature in brutal fashion take place irrespective of their location and regardless of the state forms – whether socialist, communist, or capitalist – under which they occur. While her analysis confronts us with the challenge of neoliberal globalization that will literally bring life to an end, soon, if we do not find a way to sustain, a larger challenge for Sassen is to articulate what the next economic system should look like. If it is not failed communism and unbridled capitalism, what will it look like? The question of what kind of genuinely compelling vision of human political, social, and economic arrangements would stand in opposition to the neoliberal agenda is an urgent one. In other words, at this present juncture, when the sheer complexity of the global economy makes it hard to trace lines of responsibility for destroyed economies, livelihoods, and bodies, how can we engage in resisting the social and environmental havoc wrought by financial capitalists while featuring visions of alternative arrangements? These are our challenges.

The chapter ends with an acknowledgement that there is much work still to be done on memory and migration from the perspective of colonization, refugee experience, and decolonizing performances, as well as from the perspective of the Anthropocene, remembering a future trauma in order to mitigate against climate catastrophe and global financial inequality. What are the implications of the notion of the Anthropocene for memory studies? How, if at all, does the awareness of living in a new geological epoch defined by the actions of human beings affect the objects of memory, the scales of remembrance, and the field's humanist underpinnings? Memory studies scholars such as Stef Craps (2017) and Jennifer Wenzel (2018) as well as theatre and performance studies scholars such as Baz Kershaw (2007), Vicky Angelaki

(2019), and Helen Gilbert (2020), to name just a few, have started addressing these issues especially in relation to theatre performances which foreground future-history approaches to climate change. These performances sensitize spectators to the enormity of the losses they or later generations will face if the current state of affairs continues, as well as ecological grief as an emotional experience brought on by the actual or anticipated loss of cherished natural spaces, ecosystems, and species caused by environmental change. Justin Shoulder's atmospheric piece *Carrion* (Australia, 2019), which asks what it means to be human in an era when our destructive influence over the planet is rapidly redefining the laws of nature, and contemporary dance company Marrugeku's *Cut in the Sky* (Australia, 2018), a haunting evocation of a world ravaged by the climate change, are two striking examples of the kind of work produced in this vein. I contend that in these performances, memory is mobilized in the hope of averting the catastrophe being remembered, which at the time of viewing has not yet (fully) happened. Therefore, the proleptic memory of climate catastrophe can perhaps function as a spur to action that would prevent the anticipated catastrophe from actually coming to pass.

Notes

Introduction

1   For instance, Traverso relates this turn in Western societies' memory to events such as Vichy's return to the arena of public debate as well as with the rise of Jewish memory, particularly after the release of Claude Lanzmann's *Shoah* (1985), which took place in France; the broadcasting of the American TV series *Holocaust* and then the *Historikerstreit* (1986), the 'historians' dispute' that unfolded in Germany more than three decades ago.

2   The summer of Operation Protective Edge, the 51-day Israeli siege of Gaza, was also the summer police shot Michael Brown in Ferguson, Missouri. Organizers protesting these seemingly disparate events began drawing connections between the Israeli occupation of Palestine and the militarization of police in Ferguson, with the militarized containment of civilians in Ferguson echoing those of the settler colonial occupation of Palestine (see Puar 2017: ix).

Part One

1   Independently of a query concerning the relation of memory and history in recent scholarship focusing on the twentieth century, a number of studies have attempted to place the idea of memory in historical perspective during premodern periods. Frances A. Yates' *The Art of Memory* (1966) traces transformations in *ars memoria* – the rhetorical art of memorizing through spatial images – from Roman times through the Renaissance, where the art of memory persisted

in the humanist tradition despite its decline due to the spread of the printing press. Janet Coleman's *Ancient and Medieval Memories: Studies in the Reconstruction of the Past* (1992) offers a comprehensive history of theories of memory from antiquity through later medieval times. In *The Book of Memory: A Study of Memory in Medieval Culture* (1990) and *The Craft of Thought: Meditation, Rhetoric, and the Making of Images, 400–1200* (1998), Mary Carruthers demonstrates the persistence of memory training even with the spread of texts, which resulted in the highly mixed oral-literate nature of medieval cultures. Lina Bolzoni's study *The Gallery of Memory: Literary and Iconographic Models in the Age of the Printing Press* (2001) deals with the practices related to memory in sixteenth-century culture. A number of other recent works in the field of intellectual history have attempted to grapple with the intriguing problem of the historicity of the phenomenon of memory in the West. This idea of historicity of memory has been inspired in part by Pierre Nora's essay 'Between Memory and History' (1989), which introduced the multi-volume series he directed, *Realms of Memory: Rethinking the French Past (1996–98)*. In this vein, Patrick H. Hutton's *History as an Art of Memory* (1993), Mat K. Matsuda's *The Memory of the Modern* (1996), and Richard Terdiman's *Present Past: Modernity and Memory Crisis* (1993) all centre on the historical transformations to which, according to the different perspectives of their works, 'memory has been subject'. Like Nora, they link this historicity of the social and cultural role of memory to the radical transformations that Western civilization has undergone in the modern period.

2   As Mary Carruthers also points out, 'Zeno the Stoic (4th–3rd century BC) defines memory as "*thesaurismos phantasion*" or "storehouse of mental images". *Thesaurus* is used metaphorically both in Romans (2:5) and the Gospel of Matthew (6:19–20) in the sense of storing up intangible things for salvation .... *The Rhetorica ad Herennium* calls memory the treasure house of found-things, "thesauru[s] inventorum" (iii, 16), referring particularly to a memory trained by the artificial scheme, which the author proceeds to recommend. Quintilian, also recommending a cultivated memory, calls it "*thesaurus eloquentiae*" (xi, 2, 2)' (Carruthers 1992: 34–5).

3   In recent years, critics have called attention to the limitations
     of trauma theory, claiming that notions of class, race, gender,
     and sex have not received due attention within its boundaries.
     Many of them have argued for the importance of rethinking
     trauma theory from a postcolonial perspective and the need
     to address the traumas visited upon members of non-Western
     cultures. For this critical trend in twenty-first-century trauma
     studies, see, for instance, Huyssen (2003); Bennett and Kennedy
     (2003); Hodgkin and Radstone (2003); Kaplan and Wang
     (2004); Kaplan (2005); Bennett (2005); Ball (2008); Radstone
     (2007a, 2007b, 2011); Fassin and Rechtman (2009); Rothberg
     (2009); and Craps (2013). See also the special issues of the
     journals *Life Writing* 5.1, edited by Kate Douglas, Gillian
     Whitlock, and Bettina Stumm (2008) and *Continuum* 24.1
     edited by Antonio Traverso and Mick Broderick (2008), which
     explore a wide range of uses and applications of trauma theory
     beyond the scope of the conventional theory of trauma.

4   As Craps notes, scholars such as Wendy Brown (1995) and
     Lauren Berlant (2007) have expressed strong doubts about the
     political value and efficacy of focusing on traumatic suffering,
     offering powerful critiques of the depoliticizing tendencies of
     hegemonic trauma discourses seen to privilege psychological
     recovery 'over the transformation of a wounding political, social,
     and economic system' (2013: 28). However, I would argue along
     with Craps that, though 'trauma research does not in and of itself
     lead to political transformation', it can act as an impetus for
     individuals and communities to work through their histories and
     memories of suffering and conflict from more active positions
     of political agency (2013: 126). In recent years, for instance,
     we have seen trauma discourses combined with other cultural
     strategies of working through a traumatic past that emphasize
     the establishment of truth and delivery of social and institutional
     justice, or apology, forgiveness, reconciliation, and compensation.

5   For more traditional intellectual histories that focus on the
     figure of melancholia, see Babb (1951); Jackson (1986);
     Klibansky, Panofsky, and Saxl (1964); and Wittkower (1963).
     For an assessment of the similarities and differences between
     the melancholic states of past eras and today's depression, see
     Radden (2003). On the gendered distinction between melancholia
     and depression, see Radden (1987) and Schiesari (1992).

Part Two

1   The past few decades have witnessed the publication of numerous works in the developing field of gender studies and Holocaust studies by prominent writers and academics. Dalia Ofer and Lenore Weitzman's edited collection *Women in the Holocaust* (1998) and Zoë Waxman's *Women in the Holocaust: A Feminist History* (2017) are premised on the belief that exploring gender was crucial to arriving at a richer, more nuanced understanding of the Holocaust.

Part Three

1   It was the 1971 Immigration Act that introduced the racially coded concept of partiality, which meant that only those who could prove their grandparents had been born in Britain would qualify for automatic right of abode. This effectively reclassified 'New Commonwealth' citizens as 'immigrants'.

2   As Matthew Mead notes, 'in the 1951 census the figures for population by place of birth for England and Wales show that 2,024 residents were born in British Guiana; 6,447 in Jamaica; 1,569 in Trinidad; 110,767 in India; and 11,117 in Pakistan, while the numbers for Polish-born were 151,736; for Germany 96,379; and Italy, 33,159. This broader general history evidences a certain synchronicity between Caribbean, South Asian, and European migration; a movement that was not lost on the post-war media or government' (2009: 143).

BIBLIOGRAPHY

Abraham, N. and M. Torok (1994), *The Shell and the Kernel*, trans. and ed. Nicolas T. Rand, Chicago and London: University of Chicago Press.

Abu-Lughod, L. and A. H. Sa'di (eds.) (2007), *Nakba: Palestine, 1948, and the Claims of Memory*, New York: Columbia University Press.

Agamben, G. (2015), *Stasis: Civil War as a Political Paradigm: Homo Sacer, II, 2*, trans. Nicholas Heron, Edinburgh: Edinburgh University Press.

Agnew, V. (2007), 'Historical Reenactment and Its Work in the Present', *Rethinking History*, 11 (3): 299–312.

Amálio, A. M. R. H. (2018), *Re-Writing Portuguese Recent Colonial History Through Postcolonial Documentary Theatre*, Doctoral dissertation, London: University of Roehampton.

Andermahr, S. (2019), 'Decolonizing Cultural Memory in Andrea Levy's Small Island', *Journal of Postcolonial Writing*, 55 (4): 555–69.

Anderson, D. (2005), *Histories of the Hanged: The Dirty War in Kenya and the End of Empire*, London: Weidenfeld & Nicolson.

Angelaki, V. (2019), *Theatre & Environment*, London: Palgrave.

Arendt, H. ([1951] 1973), *The Origins of Totalitarianism*, New York: Houghton Mifflin Harcourt.

Arendt, H. (1968), *The Origins of Totalitarianism*, New York: Harcourt Brace Jovanovich.

Arias, L. (2016), 'Memory Is a Minefield', STR Edward Gordon Craig Lecture, King's College, University of London, 6 June.

Arias, L. (dir.) (2016), *Minefield*, London: Royal Court Theatre. Available online: https://royalcourttheatre.com/whats-on/minefield/ (accessed 1 December 2019).

Arsenijević, D. (2014), 'Protests and Plenum: The Struggle for the Commons', in D. Arsenijević (ed.), *Unbribable Bosnia and Herzegovina: The Fight for the Commons*, 45–50, Baden: Nomos.

Arsham-Kuftinec, S. (2009), *Theatre, Facilitation, and Nation Formation in the Balkans and Middle East*, Basingstoke: Palgrave Macmillan.

Assmann, A. (2018), 'One Land and Three Narratives: Palestinian Sites of Memory in Israel', *Memory Studies*, 11 (3): 287–300.

Assmann, A. and S. Conrad (eds.) (2010), *Memory in a Global Age: Discourses, Practices and Trajectories*, Basingstoke: Palgrave Macmillan.

Athanasiou, A. (2017), *Agonistic Mourning: Political Dissidence and the Women in Black*, Edinburgh: Edinburgh University Press.

Augustine, S., Bishop of Hippo (2002), *Saint Augustine's Memory*, trans. and ed. G. Wills, New York: Viking.

Azoulay, A. (2012), *Civil Imagination: A Political Ontology of Photography*, trans. L. Bethlehem, London and New York: Verso.

Babb, L. (1951), *The Elizabethan Malady: A Study of Melancholia in English Literature from 1580–1642*, East Lansing: Michigan State College Press.

Ball, K. (2008), *Disciplining the Holocaust*, Albany: State University of New York Press.

Bender, G. (2004), *Angola under the Portuguese – The Myth and the Reality*, Trenton: África World Press.

Benhabib, S. (2004), *The Rights of Others: Aliens, Residents, and Citizens*, Cambridge: Cambridge University Press.

Benhabib, S. (2018), *Exile, Statelessness, and Migration: Playing Chess with History from Hannah Arendt to Isaiah Berlin*, Princeton and Oxford: Princeton University Press.

Benjamin, W. ([1940] 2006), 'On the Concept of History', in H. Eiland and M. W. Jennings (eds.), *Selected Writings, Vol. 4: 1938–1940*, trans. and ed. H. Zohn, 391–2, Cambridge, MA: Belknap Press.

Bennett, J. (2005), *Empathic Vision: Affect, Trauma, and Contemporary Art*, Stanford: Stanford University Press.

Bennett, J. and R. Kennedy (2003), *World Memory: Personal Trajectories in Global Time*, New York: Palgrave Macmillan.

Berlant, L. (2007), 'The Subject of True Feeling: Pain, Privacy, and Politics', in K. Ball (ed.), *Traumatizing Theory: The Cultural Politics of Affect in and beyond Psychoanalysis*, 305–47, New York: Other Press.

Bhambra, G. K. (2017), '"Our Island Story": The Dangerous Politics of Belonging in Austere Times', in S. Jonsonn and J. Willen (eds.), *Austere Histories in European Societies: Social Exclusion and the Contest of Colonial Memories*, 21–37, London: Routledge.

Biddick, K. (2007), *The Shock of Medievalism*, Durham: Duke University Press.

Bither, P. (2019), 'We Are All Writing the Novels of Our Lives: Lola Arias on War, Memory, and Documentary Theater', *Walker*. Available online: https://walkerart.org/magazine/lola-arias-minefield-documentary-theater (accessed 29 March 2020).

Blejmar, J. (2017), 'Autofictions of Postwar: Fostering Empathy in Lola Arias's *Minefield/Campo Minado*', *Journal of Latin American Studies*, 50 (2) (Spring): 103–23.

Bolzoni, L. (2001), *The Gallery of Memory: Literary and Iconographic Models in the Age of the Printing Press*, Toronto: University of Toronto Press.

Brown, L. S. (2008), *Cultural Competence in Trauma Therapy: Beyond the Flashback*, Washington, DC: American Psychological Association.

Brown, J.D. and L.R. Rosenberg (2015), *Beyond Windrush: Rethinking Postwar Anglophone Caribbean literature*, Jackson: University Press of Mississippi.

Brown, W. (1995), *States of Injury: Power and Freedom in Late Modernity*, Princeton: Princeton University Press.

Brown, W. (2019), *In the Ruins of Neoliberalism: The Rise of Antidemocratic Politics in the West*, New York: Columbia University Press.

Brustein, R. (1997), 'The Journey of Robert Lepage', *The New Republic,* 10 February, 29–31.

Butler, J. (1997a), *Excitable Speech: Politics of the Performative*, New York: Routledge.

Butler, J. (1997b), *The Psychic Life of Power: Theories of Subjection*, Stanford: Stanford University Press.

Butler, J. (2004), *Precarious Life: The Powers of Mourning and Violence*, London; New York: Verso.

Butler, J. (2005), *Giving an Account of Oneself*, New York: Fordham University Press.

Carlson, M. (2003), *The Haunted Stage: The Theatre as Memory Machine*, Ann Arbor: University of Michigan Press.

Carruthers, M. J. (1992), *The Book of Memory: A Study of Memory in Medieval Culture*, Cambridge: Cambridge University Press.

Carruthers, M. J. (1998), *The Craft of Thought: Meditation, Rhetoric, and the Making of Images*, Cambridge: Cambridge University Press.

Caruth, C. (1995), 'Introduction', in C. Caruth (ed.), *Trauma: Explorations in Memory*, 3–12; 151–7, Baltimore: Johns Hopkins University Press.

Caruth, C. (1996), *Unclaimed Experience: Trauma, Narrative and History*, Baltimore: Johns Hopkins University Press.

Caruth, C. (2017), '"A Perverse Quest for Meaning": False Witness in Vietnam and Beyond', *Continuum*, 31 (5): 610–18.

CDC (2019), 'HIV in the United States: At a Glance', Centers for Disease Control and Prevention, December. Available online: https://www.cdc.gov/hiv/statistics/overview/ataglance.html (accessed 10 February 2020).

Chambers, R. (2004), *Untimely Interventions: Aids Writing, Testimonial, and the Rhetoric of Haunting*, Ann Arbor: University of Michigan Press.

Cherkaev, Xenia (2014), 'On Warped Mourning and Omissions in Post-Soviet Historiography', *Ab Imperio*, 4: 365–85.

Choksey, L. (2019), 'Windrush, Welfare and Caring for History', *Media Diversified*, 17 April. Available online: https://mediadiversified.org/2019/04/17/windrush-welfare-and-caring-for-history (accessed 1 December 2019).

Cole, C. M. (2010), *Performing South Africa's Truth Commission: Stages of Transition*, Bloomington: Indiana University Press.

Coleman, J. (1992), *Ancient and Medieval Memories: Studies in the Reconstruction of the Past*, Cambridge: Cambridge University Press.

Confino, A. (2016), 'The Holocaust and the Nakba (Review of Bashir, Goldberg)', *H-soz-kult*. Available online: https://www.hsozkult.de/publicationreview/id/rezbuecher-25731 (accessed 14 November 2019).

Cox, E. (2014), *Theatre and Migration*, Houndmills, Basingstoke, Hampshire; New York: Palgrave Macmillan.

Cox, E. (2015), *Performing Noncitizenship: Asylum Seekers in Australian Theatre, Film and Activism*, New York: Anthem Press.

Cox, E. and C. Wake (2018), 'Envisioning Asylum/Engendering Crisis: Or, Performance and Forced Migration 10 Years On', *Research in Drama Education*, 23 (2): 137–47.

Craps, S. (2010), 'Wor(l)ds of Grief: Traumatic Memory and Literary Witnessing in Cross-Cultural Perspective', *Textual Practice*, 24 (1): 51–68.

Craps, S. (2013), *Postcolonial Witnessing: Trauma Out of Bounds*. Basingstoke; New York: Palgrave Macmillan.

Craps, S. (2017), 'Climate Change and the Art of Anticipatory Memory', *Parallax*, 23 (4): 479–92.

Cummings, S. T. (1997), 'The Seven Streams of River Ota by Robert Lepage Review', *Theatre Journal*, 49 (3): 348–52.

Darian-Smith, K. and P. Hamilton (eds.) (2019), *Remembering Migration: Oral Histories and Heritage in Australia*, Cham, Switzerland: Palgrave Macmillan.

Dear, M. J. (2015), *Why Walls Won't Work: Repairing the US-Mexico Divide*, New York: Oxford University Press.

Delgado, M. M. (2019), 'Ways of Remembering Las Malvinas/The Falklands', in J. Graham-Jones (ed.), *Lola Arias: Re-enacting Life*, 1–14, New York: Centre For Performance Research.

Ribeiro de Menezes, A. (2016), 'Out of the Labyrinth? Television Memories of Revolution and Return in Contemporary Portugal', *Journal of Romance Studies*, 16 (2): 76–95.

Santos, B. S. (2009), 'Portugal: Tales of Being and Not-Being', *Portuguese Literary and Cultural Studies*, 20(19): 1–46.

Douglas, K., G. Whitlock and B. Stumm (2008), 'Trauma in the Twenty-First Century', *Life Writing*, 5 (1): 1–8.

Dwork, D. and R. J. Van Pelt (2009), *Flight for the Reich: Refugee Jews, 1933–1946*, New York; London: W. W. Norton.

Elkins, C. (2005), *Imperial Reckoning: The Untold Story of Britain's Gulag in Kenya*, New York: Henry Holt.

Enders, J. (1999), *The Medieval Theatre of Cruelty: Rhetoric, Memory, Violence*, Ithaca and London: Cornell University Press.

Eng, D. L. (2016), 'Colonial Object Relations', *Social Text*, 34.1 (126): 1–19.

Engelking, B. (2001), *Holocaust and Memory. The Experience of the Holocaust and Its Consequences: An Investigation Based on Personal Narratives*, trans. E. Harris, ed. G. S. Paulsson, London: Leicester University Press.

Erll, A. and A. Rigney (eds.) (2018), 'Cultural Memory Studies after the Transnational Turn', *Memory Studies*, 11 (3): 272–385.

Estrada Fuentes, M. (2017), 'Becoming Citizens: Loss and Desire in the Social Reintegration of Guerrilla Ex-Combatants in

Colombia', in J. Reinelt, B. Dutt and, S. Sahai (eds.), *Gendered Citizenship: Manifestations and Performance*, 271–90, Cham: Springer International Publishing AG.

Etkind, A. (2013), *Warped Mourning: Stories of the Undead in the Land of the Unburied*, Stanford, CA: Stanford University Press.

Fassin, D. and R. Rechtman (2009), *The Empire of Trauma: An Inquiry into the Condition of Victimhood*, trans. R. Gomme, Princeton: Princeton University Press.

Ferguson, N. (2003), *Empire: How Britain Made the Modern World*, London: Allen Lane.

Finburgh, C. (2017), '"Violence without Violence": Spectacle, War and Lola Arias's MINEFIELD/CAMPO MINADO', *Theatre Research International*, 42 (2): 163–78.

Fleishman, M. (2015), *Performing Migrancy and Mobility in Africa: Cape of Flows*, Palgrave Macmillan.

Flockhart, S. (2018), 'Bakira Hasečić: My Crusade to Bring Those Who Raped Me and Killed My Friends to Justice', *The Herald*, 8 July. Available online: https://www.heraldscotland.com/news/16340348.bakira-hasečić-my-crusade-to-bring-those-who-raped-me-and-killed-my-friends-to-justice (accessed 29 March 2020).

Freud, S. ([1915] 1957), 'On Transience', in James Strachey (trans. and ed.), *The Standard Edition of the Complete Psychological Works of Sigmund Freud*, Vol. 14, 303–7, London: Hogarth Press.

Freud, S. ([1917] 1957), 'Mourning and Melancholia', in James Strachey (trans. and ed.), *The Standard Edition of the Complete Psychological Works of Sigmund Freud*, Vol. 14, 243–58, London: Hogarth Press.

Freud, S. ([1923] 1955), 'The Ego and the Id', in James Strachey (trans. and ed.), *The Standard Edition of the Complete Psychological Works of Sigmund Freud*, Vol. 19, 1–59, London: Hogarth Press.

Freud, S. ([1938] 1966), 'The Splitting of the Ego as a Mechanism of Defence', in J. Strachey (trans. and ed.), *The Standard Edition of the Complete Psychological Works of Sigmund Freud*, Vol. 23, London: Hogarth Press, 271–8.

Fricker, K. (2003), 'The Festival Marketplace and Robert Lepage's The Seven Streams of the River Ota', *Contemporary Theatre Review*, 13 (4): 79–93.

Fricker, K. (2020), *Robert Lepage's Original Stage Productions: Making Theatre Global*, Manchester: Manchester University Press.

Fricker, K. and M. Gluhovic (2013), *Performing the 'New' Europe: Identities, Feelings and Politics in the Eurovision Song Contest*, New York: Palgrave Macmillan.

Garelli, G., A. Sciurba, and M. Tazzioli (2018), 'Introduction: Mediterranean Movements in 2015 and the Reconfiguration of the Military-Humanitarian Border', *Antipode*, 50 (3): 662–72.

Gentleman, A. (2019), *The Windrush Betrayal: Exposing the Hostile Environment*, London: Guardian Faber Publishing.

Gilbert, H. (2020), 'Performing the Anthropocene: Marrugeku's Cut the Sky', in B. Neumeier and H. Tiffin (eds.), *Ecocritical Concerns and the Australian Continent*, 219–34, Lanham, MD: Lexington Books.

Glissant, É. (1989), *Caribbean Discourse: Selected Essays*, trans. J. M. Dash, Charlottesville, VA: University of Virginia Press.

Gluhovic, M. (2008), 'Too Distant Shores: The Strait of Gibraltar and the Space of Exception', *Research in Drama Education: The Journal of Applied Theatre and Performance*, 13 (2): 147–58.

Grace, S. (2006), 'Playing Butterfly with David Henry Hwang and Robert Lepage', in J. L. Wisenthal (ed.), *A Vision of the Orient: Texts, Intertexts, and Contexts of Madame Butterfly*, i–xiii, Toronto: University of Toronto Press.

Hájková, A. (2013), 'Sexual Barter in Times of Genocide: Negotiating the Sexual Economy of the *Theresienstadt* Ghetto', *Signs*, 38 (3): 503–33.

Hájková, A. (2020), *The Last Ghetto: An Everyday History of Theresienstadt*, Oxford: Oxford University Press.

Hall, C. (2020), 'Mother Country', *London Review of Books*, 42 (2). Available online: https://www.lrb.co.uk/the-paper/v42/n02/catherine-hall/mother-country/ (accessed 26 April 2020).

Hall, S. (1991), 'Reconstruction Work: Images of Post-War Black Settlement', in J. Spence and P. Holland (eds.), *Family Snaps: The Meanings of Domestic Photography*, 152–64, London: Virago.

Hartman, S. (2002), 'The Time of Slavery', *The South Atlantic Quarterly*, 101 (4): 757–77.

Hirsch, M. (1999), 'Projected Memory: Holocaust Photographs in Personal and Public Fantasy', in M. Bal, J. Crew, and L. Spitzer (eds.), *Acts of Memory: Cultural Recall in the Present*, 3–23, Hanover and London: University Press of New England.

Hirsch, M. (2012), *The Generation of Postmemory: Writing and Visual Culture after the Holocaust*, New York: Columbia University Press.

Hirsch, M. (2019), 'Introduction: Practicing Feminism, Practicing Memory', in B. Karaca, J. Howard, M. Hirsch, M. J. Contreras, A. G. Altınay, and A. Solomon (eds.), *Women Mobilizing Memory*, 1–23, New York: Columbia University Press.

Hirsch, M. and L. Spitzer (2009), 'The Witness in the Archive: Holocaust Studies/ Memory Studies', *Memory Studies*, 2 (2): 151–70.

Hirsch, M. and L. Spitzer (2010), *Ghosts of Home: The Afterlife of Czernowitz in Jewish Memory*, Berkeley: University of California Press.

Hirsch, M. and L. Spitzer (2017), 'Small Acts of Repair: The Unclaimed Legacy of the Romanian Holocaust', in L. Bond, S. Craps, and P. Vermeulen (eds.), *Memory Unbound: Tracing the Dynamics of Memory Studies*, 83–109, New York: Berghahn Books.

Hodgkin, K. and S. Radstone (eds.) (2003), *Contested Pasts: The Politics of Memory*, New York and London: Routledge.

Hodgkin, K. and S. Radstone (eds.) (2006), *Memory, History, Nation: Contested Pasts*, New Brunswick: Transaction.

Horvat, S. and I. Štiks (eds.) (2014), *Welcome to the Desert of Post-Socialism*, London, New York: Verso.

Hutchison, Y. (2013), *South African Performance and Archives of Memory*, Manchester and New York: Manchester University Press.

Hutton, P. H. (1993), *History as an Art of Memory*, Hanover and London: University Press of New England.

Huyssen, A. (2003), 'Rewritings and New Beginnings: W. G. Sebald and the Literature on the Air War', in *Present Past: Urban Palimpsests and the Politics of Memory*, 138–57, Stanford, CA: Stanford University Press.

IOM (2017), 'Migrant Deaths and Disappearances Worldwide: 2016 Analysis', *International Organization for Migration*, Data Briefing Series, Issue No. 8, 8 March. Available online: https://gmdac.iom.int/gmdac-data-briefing-8 (accessed 1 December 2019).

Jackson, S. W. (1986), *Melancholia and Depression: From Hippocratic Times to Modern Times*, New Haven: Yale University Press.

Lifton, R. J. (1967), *Death in Life: Survivors in Hiroshima*, New York: Basic Books.

Jerónimo, M. B. (2015), *The 'Civilizing Mission' of Portuguese Colonialism, 1870–1930*, trans. S. Lloyd-Jone, rev. M. Fino Jeronimo and M. Bandeira Jeronimo, Houndmills, Basingstoke, Hampshire: Palgrave Macmillan.

Jestrović, S. (2019), 'Bringing the Left Back: Radical Performances of Dissent from the Remains of ex-Yugoslavia', *Studies in Theatre and Performance*, 39 (3): 1–16.

Jones, A. (2011), '"The Artist Is Present": Artistic Re-enactments and the Impossibility of Presence', *TDR: The Drama Review*, 55 (1): 16–45.

Kantor, T. (1983), *Wielopole, Wielopole*, dir. A. Zajączkowski, Krakow: OTV Kraków.

Kantor, T. (1984), *Wielopole, Wielopole*, dir. A. Sapija, W.F.O. Łódz.

Kantor, T. (1990a), *Wielopole Wielopole*, trans. M. Tchorek and G. M. Hyde, London and New York: Marion Boyars.

Kantor, T. (1990b), *The Theatre of Death and Love, Cricot 2 Theatre – Information Guide 1989–1990*, ed. A. Halczak, Cracow: Cricoteka.

Kantor, T. (1993), *A Journey through Other Spaces: Essays and Manifestos, 1944–1990*, trans. and ed. M. Kobialka, Berkeley: University of California Press.

Kaplan, E. A. (2005), *Trauma Culture: The Politics of Terror and Loss in Media and Literature*, New Brunswick, New Jersey, and London: Rutgers University Press.

Kaplan, E. A. (2016), *Climate Trauma: Foreseeing the Future in Dystopian Film and Fiction*, New Brunswick and New Jersey: Rutgers University Press.

Kaplan, E. A. and B. Wang (eds.) (2004), *Trauma and Cinema: Cross-cultural Explorations (Vol. 1)*, Hong Kong: Hong Kong University Press.

Kapoor, N. (2018), *Deport, Deprive, Extradite: 21st Century State Extremism*, London: Verso.

Kershaw, B. (2007), *Theatre Ecology: Environments and Performance Events*, Cambridge: Cambridge University Press.

Khanna, R. (2003), *Dark Continents: Psychoanalysis and Colonialism*, Durham, NC: Duke University Press.

Khouri, E. (2018), 'Foreword', in A. Goldberg and B. Bashir (eds.), *The Holocaust and the Nabka: A New Grammar of Trauma and History*, ix–xvi, New York: Columbia University Press.

Klein, M. ([1937] 1975), 'Love, Guilt, and Reparation', in M. Klein (ed.), *Love, Guilt and Reparation and Other Works 1921–1945 (The Writings of Melanie Klein, Volume 1)*, 306–69, New York: Free Press.

Klein, M. (1986), 'Mourning and Its Relation to Manic-Depressive States', in J. Mitchell (ed.), *The Selected Melanie Klein*, 146–74, New York: Free Press.

Klibansky, R., E. Panofsky, and F. Saxl. (1964), *Saturn and Melancholy: Studies on the History of Natural Philosophy, Religion, and Art*, London: Thomas Nelson and Sons.

Knowles, R. (2000), 'The Edinburgh Festival and Fringe: Lessons for Canada?', *Canadian Theatre Review*, 102 (Spring): 88–96.

Kouvelakis, S. (2018), 'Borderland: Greece and the EU's Southern Question', *New Left Review*, 110 (March/April): 5–32.

Kristeva, J. (1989), *Black Sun: Depression and Melancholia*, trans. L. S. Roudiez, New York: Columbia University Press.

Kushner, T. (2017), *Journeys from the Abyss: The Holocaust and Forced Migration from the 1880s to the Present*, Liverpool: Liverpool University Press.

Lachmann, R. (1997), *Memory and Literature: Intersexuality in Russian Modernism*. Minneapolis: University of Minnesota Press.

Lai, D. and C. Bonora (2019), 'The Transformative Potential of Post-war Justice Initiatives in Bosnia and Herzegovina', in M. Evans (ed.), *Transitional and Transformative Justice: Critical and International Perspectives*, 54–76, New York: Routledge.

Lammy, D. (2018), 'Perspectives on the Windrush Generation Scandal: A Response from David Lammy MP', *British Library*, 4 October. Available online: https://www.bl.uk/windrush/articles/ perspectives-on-the-windrush-generation-scandal-a-response- from-david-lammy (accessed 1 December 2019).

Laub, D. (1992), 'An Event without a Witness, Truth, Testimony and Survival', in S. Felman and D. Laub (eds.), *Testimony: Crisis of Witnessing in Literature, Psychoanalysis, and History*, 75–92, New York: Routledge.

Lehmann, H. T. (2006), *Postdramatic Theatre*, trans. Karen Jürs- Munby, London; New York: Routledge.

Lehmann, R. (2001), *Symbiosis and Ambivalence: Poles and Jews in a Small Galician Town*, New York: Berghahn Books.

Lepage, R. (1996), *Seven Streams of the River Ota with an Introduction and Commentary by Karen Fricker*, ed. E. Bernier et al., London: Methuen Drama, Bloomsbury.

Levi, N. and M. Rothberg (2018), 'Memory Studies in a Moment of Danger: Fascism, Postfascism, and the Contemporary Political Imaginary', *Memory Studies*, 11 (3), 355–67.

Levy, A. (2004), *Small Island*, London: Headline Review.

Levy, A. (2019), *Small Island*, adapted for the stage by Helen Edmundson, London: Nick Hern Books.

Levy, D. and N. Sznaider (2006), *The Holocaust and Memory in a Global Age: Politics, History, and Social Change*, Philadelphia, PA: Temple University Press.

Lifton, R. J. ([1973] 1992), *Home from the War: Learning from Vietnam Veterans*, Boston, MA: Beacon Press.

Looser, D. (2014), *Remaking Pacific Pasts: History, Memory, and Identity in Contemporary Theater from Oceania*, Honolulu: University of Hawai'i Press.

Lubkemann, S. C. (2003), 'Race, Class and Kin in the Negotiation of 'Internal Strangerhood' among Portuguese Retornados, 1975–2000', in A. L. Smith (ed.), *Europe's Invisible Migrants*, 75–93, Amsterdam: Amsterdam University Press.

Maclear, K. (1998), *Beclouded Visions: Hiroshima-Nagasaki and the Art of Witness*, New York: State University of New York Press.

Macmillan, D. (2014), *The Forbidden Zone*, unpublished manuscript.

Malkin, J. R. (1999), *Memory-Theatre and Postmodern Drama*, Ann Arbor: University of Michigan Press.

Matsuda, M. K. (1996), *The Memory of the Modern*, Oxford: Oxford University Press.

Mead, M. (2009), 'Empire Windrush: The Cultural Memory of an Imaginary Arrival', *Journal of Postcolonial Writing*, 45 (2): 137–49.

Merridale, C. (2010), 'Soviet Memories: Patriotism and Trauma', in S. Radstone and B. Schwarz (eds.), *Memory: Histories, Theories, Debates*, 376–90, New York: Fordham University Press.

Milan, C. (2017), '"Sow Hunger, Reap Anger": From Neoliberal Privatization to New Collective Identities in Bosnia-Herzegovina', in D. Della Porta (ed.), *Global Diffusion of Protest: Riding the Protest Wave in the Neoliberal Crisis*, 167–90, Amsterdam: Amsterdam University Press.

Mitchell, K. (dir.) (2014), *The Forbidden Zone*, Berlin: Schaubuhne Berlin. Available online: https://59productions.co.uk/project/forbidden-zone/ (accessed 1 December 2019).

Mogherini, F. (2015), 'Keynote Speech for the ISPI Dinner at the Conference "Mediterranean Dialogue" in Rome', *federicamogherini.net*, 11 December. Available online: http://www.federicamogherini.net/keynote-speech-for-the-ispi-dinner-at-the-conference-mediterranean-dialogue-rome/ (accessed 1 December 2019).

Morefield, J. (2014), *Empires without Imperialism: Anglo-American Decline and the Politics of Deflection*, Oxford: Oxford University Press.

Morier-Genoud, E. and M. Cahen (eds.) (2012), *Imperial Migrations: Colonial Communities and Diaspora in the Portuguese World*, Basingstoke: Palgrave Macmillan.

Moses, D. A. (2011), 'Genocide and the Terror of History', *parallax*, 17 (4): 90–108.

Moses, D. and M. Rothberg (2014), 'A Dialogue on the Ethics and Politics of Transcultural Memory', in L. Bond and J. Rapson (eds.), *The Transcultural Turn : Interrogating Memory between and beyond Borders, Media and Cultural Memory*, 29–38, Berlin: De Gruyter.

Naimark, N. M. (1995), *The Russians in Germany: A History of the Soviet Zone of Occupation, 1945–1949*, Cambridge, MA; London: Belknap Press of Harvard University Press.

Naimark, N. M. (2009), 'Srebrenica in the History of Genocide: A Prologue', in N. Adler et al. (eds.), *Memories of Mass Repression: Narrating Life Stories in the Aftermath of Atrocity*, 3–20, New Brunswick, NJ: Transaction Publishers.

Nora, P. (1989), 'Between Memory and History: Les lieux de mémoire', *Representations*, 26 (7): 24.

Nora, P. (1996–8), *Realms of Memory: Rethinking the French Past*, New York: Columbia University Press.

Nyong'o, T. (2019), 'Does Staging Historical Trauma Reenact It?', in M. Bleeker, A. Kear, J. Kelleher, and H. Roms (eds.), *Thinking Through Theatre and Performance*, 200–10, London: Methuen Drama, Bloomsbury.

Ofer, D. and L. J. Weitzman (eds.) (1998), *Women in the Holocaust*, New Haven: Yale University Press.

Ovalle-Bahamón, R. E. (2003), 'The Wrinkles of Decolonization and Nationness: White Angolans as Retornados in Portugal', in

A. L. Smith (ed.), *Europe's Invisible Migrants*, 147–68, Amsterdam: Amsterdam University Press.

Patočka, J. (1996), *Heretical Essays in the Philosophy of History (with Paul Ricoeur's preface to the French edition)*, ed. J. Dodd, trans. E. Kohák, Chicago: Open Court.

Paxman, J. (2011), *Empire: What Ruling the World Did to the British*, London: Viking, Penguin Group.

Peschel, L. (ed.) (2014), *Performing Captivity, Performing Escape: Cabarets and Plays from Terezín/Theresienstadt Ghetto*, London: Seagull Books.

Pleśniarowicz, K. (2004), *The Dead Memory Machine: Tadeusz Kantor's Theatre of Death*, trans. W. Brand, Aberystwyth: Black Mountain Press.

Puar, J. K. (2015a), 'Inhumanist Occupation: Palestine and the "Right to Maim"', *GLQ: A Journal of Lesbian and Gay Studies*, 21 (2): 218–21.

Puar, J. K. (2015b), 'The "Right" to Maim: Disablement and Inhumanist Biopolitics in Palestine', *Borderlands*, 14 (1): 1–27.

Puar, J. K. (2017), *The Right to Maim: Debility, Capacity, Disability*, Durham: Duke University Press.

Quintilian ([1920] 1980), *Institutio oratoria*, trans. and ed. H. E. Butler, Cambridge: Harvard University Press.

Radden, J. (1987), 'Melancholy and Melancholia', in D. M. Levin (ed.), *Pathologies of the Modern Self: Postmodern Studies on Narcissism, Schizophrenia, and Depression*, 231–50, New York: New York University Press.

Radden, J. (2003), 'Is This Dame Melancholy? Equating Today's Depression and Past Melancholia', *Philosophy, Psychiatry, & Psychology*, 10 (1): 37–52.

Radstone, S. (2007a), 'Trauma Theory: Contexts, Politics, Ethics', *Paragraph*, 30 (1): 9–29.

Radstone, S. (2007b), 'Theory and Affect: Undivided Worlds', in Perri 6, S. Radstone, C. Squire, and A. Treacher (eds.), *Public Emotions*, 181–201, London: Palgrave Macmillan.

Radstone, S. (2008), 'Memory Studies: For and Against', *Journal of Memory Studies*, 1 (1): 31–9.

Radstone, S. (2011), 'What Place is This? Transcultural Memory and the Locations of Memory Studies', *Parallax*, 17 (4): 109–23.

Radstone, S. (2017), 'Sea Passages: Trauma, Arendtian Thinking and What Dialogues with Art Can Do', *Continuum*, 31 (5): 648–59.

Reinelt, J. G. (forthcoming), 'Politics Populism Performance', unpublished essay.

Richards, S. (2005), 'What Is to Be Remembered?: Tourism to Ghana's Slave Castle-Dungeons', *Theatre Journal*, 57 (4): 617–37.

Ricoeur, P. (2004), *Memory, History, Forgetting*, trans. by K. Blamey and D. Pellauer, Chicago, IL: University of Chicago Press.

Rigney, A. (2012), 'Reconciliation and Remembering: (How) Does It Work?', *Memory Studies*, 5 (3): 251–8.

Robbins, B. (2017), *The Beneficiary*, Durham: Duke University Press.

Rokem, F. (2000), *Performing History: Theatrical Representations of the Past in Contemporary Theatre*, Iowa City: University of Iowa Press.

Román, D. (1998), *Acts of Intervention: Performance, Gay Culture and AIDS*, Bloomington: Indiana University Press.

Román, D. (2015), 'The Normal Heart, Then and Now', in J. D. Katz and R. Hushka (eds.), *ArtAIDSAmerica*, 120–7, Seattle: Tacoma Art Museum in Association with University of Washington Press.

Ronen, Y. (dir.) (2014), *Common Ground*, Berlin: Gorki Theatre. Available online: https://gorki.de/en/common-ground (accessed 1 December 2019).

Ronen, Y. et al. (2014), *Common Ground*, Berlin: Gorki Theatre, unpublished manuscript.

Rothberg, M. (2009), *Multidirectional Memory: Remembering the Holocaust in the Age of Decolonization*, Stanford: Stanford University Press.

Rothberg, M. (2019), *The Implicated Subject: Beyond Victims and Perpetrators*, Stanford, CA: Stanford University Press.

Sanyal, D. (2017), 'Calais's "Jungle" – Refugees, Biopolitics, and the Arts of Resistance', *Representations*, 139 (1): 1–33.

Sassen, S. (2014), *Expulsions: Brutality and Complexity in the Global Economy*, Cambridge, MA: Harvard University Press.

Sassen, S. (2016), 'At the Systemic Edge: Expulsions', *European Review*, 24 (1): 89–104.

Schechner, R. (1985), *Between Theater & Anthropology*, Philadelphia: University of Pennsylvania.

Schiesari, J. (1992), *The Gendering of Melancholia: Feminism, Psychoanalysis, and the Symbolics of Loss in Renaissance Literature*, Ithaca: Cornell University Press.

Schneider, R. (2011), *Performing Remains: Art and War in Times of Theatrical Reenactment*, New York: Routledge.

Schneider, R. (2018), 'That the Past May yet Have Another Future: Gesture in the Times of Hands Up', *Theatre Journal*, 70 (3): 285–306.

Smith, A. L. (2003), 'Introduction: Europe's Invisible Migrants', in A. L. Smith (ed.), *Europe's Invisible Migrants*, 9–32, Amsterdam: Amsterdam University Press.

Solomon, A. (2018), 'Who Knows Where or When? AIDS and Theatrical Memory in Queer Time', *Theater*, 48 (3): 3–21.

Sosa, C. (2017), '*Campo Minado/Minefield*: War, Affect and Vulnerability – A Spectacle of Intimate Power', *Theatre Research International*, 42 (2): 179–89.

Stauffer, J. (2015), *Ethical Loneliness: The Injustice of Not Being Heard*, New York: Columbia University Press.

Stone, D. (2018), 'Refugees Then and Now: Memory, History and Politics in the Long Twentieth Century: An Introduction', *Patterns of Prejudice*, 52 (2–3): 101–6.

Stover, E. (2004), 'Witnesses and the Promise of Justice in The Hague', in E. Stover and H. M. Weinstein (eds.), *My Neighbor, My Enemy: Justice and Community in the Aftermath of Mass Atrocity*, 104–20, Cambridge: Cambridge University Press.

Taylor, D. (2003), *The Archive and the Repertoire: Performing Cultural Memory in the Americas*, Durham: Duke University Press.

Taylor, D. (2006), 'Trauma and Performance: Lessons from Latin America', *PMLA*, 121 (5): 1674–7.

Terdiman, R. (1993), *Present Past: Modernity and the Memory Crisis*, Ithaca: Cornell University Press.

Thibaudat, J. (2003), 'Kantor Will Never Return to Wielopole', in A. Halczak (ed.), *Cricot 2 Theatre Information Guide, 1989–1990*, 183–4, Kraków: Cricoteca.

Staff, T. (2019), 'The Real Winners of 2nd Eurovision Semifinal? Shalva Band Wows the World', *Times of Israel*, 17 May. Available online: https://www.timesofisrael.com/the-real-winners-of-the-second-eurovision-semifinal-shalva-band-wows-the-world/ (accessed 1 December 2019).

Traverso, E. (2016), *Left-Wing Melancholia: Marxism, History, and Memory*, New York: Columbia University Press.

Traverso, E. (2019), *The New Faces of Fascism: Populism and the Far Right*, London: Verso.

Traverso, A. and M. Broderick (2010), 'Interrogating Trauma: Towards a Critical Trauma Studies', *Continuum*, 24 (1): 3–15.

UNAIDS (2019), 'Fact Sheet – World AIDS Day 2019', *Joint United Nations Programme on HIV/AIDS*, 1 December. Available online: https://www.unaids.org/sites/default/files/media_asset/UNAIDS_FactSheet_en.pdf (accessed 10 February 2020).

UNHCR (2012), 'Mediterranean Takes Record as Most Deadly Stretch of Water for Refugees and Migrants in 2011', *United Nations High Commissioner for Refugees*, 31 January. Available online: https://www.unhcr.org/uk/news/briefing/2012/1/4f27e01f9/mediterranean-takes-record-deadly-stretch-water-refugees-migrants-2011.html (accessed 1 December 2019).

UNHCR (2017), 'Global Trends: Forced Displacement in 2016'. Available online: http://www.unhcr.org/5943e8a34.pdf. (accessed 18 October 2018).

Van Alphen, E. (2005), *'Playing the Holocaust' Art in Mind: How Contemporary Images Shape Thought*, Chicago: Chicago University Press.

Vardoulakis, D. (2018), *Stasis before the State: Nine Theses on Agonistic Democracy*, US: Fordham University Press.

Walsh, F. (2019), 'Contagious Performance: Between Illness and Ambience', in F. Walsh (ed.), *Theatres of Contagion Transmitting Early Modern to Contemporary Performance*, 3–20, London: Methuen Drama, Bloomsbury.

Waxman, Z. (2017), *Women in the Holocaust: A Feminist History*, Oxford: Oxford University Press.

Wenzel, J. (2018), '"We Have Been Thrown Away": Surplus People Projects and the Logics of Waste', *Social Dynamics*, 44 (2): 184–97.

Wieviorka, A. (2006), *The Era of Witness*, trans. Jared Stark, Ithaca: Cornell University Press.

Wilmer, S. E. (2018), *Performing Statelessness in Europe*, Cham: Palgrave Macmillan.

Wittkower, R. and M. Wittkower (1963), *Born under Saturn. The Character and Conduct of Artists: A Documented History from Antiquity to the French Revolution*, New York: Random House.

Wolff, S. and L. Hadj-Abdou (2018), 'Mediterranean Migrants and Refugees: Historical and Political Continuities and Discontinuities', in R. Gillespie, V. Frederic, and O. Abingdon (eds.), *Routledge Handbook of Mediterranean Politics*, 382–93, New York: Routledge.

Women's Court (2011), *Ženski Sud feministicki pristup pravdi* [*Women's Court, a Feministic Approach to Justice*], Belgrade: Art Print Novi Sad/Women in Black Belgrade and Centre for Women's Studies.

Women's Court, Judicial Council (2015), 'Preliminary Decisions and Recommendations, Delivered in Sarajevo, 9 May 2015', *Women's Court*. Available online: http://www.zenskisud.org/en/pdf/2015/ Womens_Court_Preliminary_Decision_Judicial_Council_2015. pdf (accessed 1 December 2019).

Women's Court, Judicial Council (n.d.), 'Ženski Sud. Feministicki pristup pravdi' ['Women's Court. A Feminist Approach to Justice']', *Women's Court*. Available online: https://www. zenskisud.org/en/pdf/RULES_Womens_Court.pdf (accessed 1 December 2019).

Yates, F. A. (1966), *The Art of Memory*, London: Routledge and Kegan Paul.

Žižek, S. (2014), 'Anger in Bosnia, but This Time the People Read Their Leaders' Ethnic Lies', *The Guardian*, 10 February. Available online: https://www.theguardian.com/commentisfree/2014/feb/10/ anger-bosnia-ethnic-lies-protesters-bosnian-serb-croat (accessed 26 April 2020).

Zwigenberg, R. (2014), *Hiroshima: The Origins of Global Memory Culture*, Cambridge: Cambridge University Press.

Further Reading

If you would like to explore further, here are some key texts to help you make a start. Some readings have been referenced in this book, while others are new.

Art of Memory/History of Memory

Bolzoni, L. (2001), *The Gallery of Memory: Literary and Iconographic Models in the Age of the Printing Press*, Toronto: University of Toronto Press.

Carruthers, M. J. (1992), *The Book of Memory: A Study of Memory in Medieval Culture*, Cambridge: Cambridge University Press.

Coleman, J. (1992), *Ancient and Medieval Memories: Studies in the Reconstruction of the Past*, Cambridge: Cambridge University Press.

Radstone, S. and B. Schwarz (eds.) (2010), *Memory: Histories, Theories, Debates*, New York: Fordham University Press.

Terdiman, R. (1993), *Present Past: Modernity and the Memory Crisis*, Ithaca: Cornell University Press.

Yates, F. A. (1966), *The Art of Memory*, London: Routledge and Kegan Paul.

Memory and Theatre and Performance Studies

Carlson, M. (2003), *The Haunted Stage: The Theatre as Memory Machine*, Ann Arbor: University of Michigan Press.

Cole, C. M. (2010), *Performing South Africa's Truth Commission: Stages of Transition*, Bloomington: Indiana University Press.

Diggs Colbert, S. (2011), *The African American Theatrical Body: Reception, Performance, and the Stage*, Cambridge: Cambridge University Press.

Enders, J. (1999), *The Medieval Theatre of Cruelty: Rhetoric, Memory, Violence*, Ithaca and London: Cornell University Press.

Malkin, J. R. (1999), *Memory-Theatre and Postmodern Drama*, Ann Arbor: University of Michigan Press.

Roach, J. R. (1996), *Cities of the Dead: Circum-Atlantic Performance*. New York: Columbia University Press.

Rokem, F. (2000), *Performing History: Theatrical Representations of the Past in Contemporary Theatre*, Iowa City: University of Iowa Press.

Schneider, R. (2011), *Performing Remains: Art and War in Times of Theatrical Reenactment*, New York: Routledge.

Taylor, D. (2003), *The Archive and the Repertoire: Performing Cultural Memory in the Americas*, Durham: Duke University Press.

Memory, Trauma, Loss

Caruth, C. (ed.) (1995), *Trauma: Explorations in Memory*, Baltimore: Johns Hopkins University Press.

Caruth, C. (1996), *Unclaimed Experience: Trauma, Narrative and History*, Baltimore: Johns Hopkins University Press.

Cheng, A. A. (2001), *The Melancholy of Race: Psychoanalysis, Assimilation, and Hidden Grief*, Oxford: Oxford University Press.

Craps, S. (2013), *Postcolonial Witnessing: Trauma out of Bounds*, Basingstoke; New York: Palgrave Macmillan.

Eng, D. L. and D. Kazanjian (eds.) (2003), *Loss: The Politics of Mourning*, Berkeley, CA; London: University of California Press.

Fassin, D. and R. Rechtman (2009), *The Empire of Trauma: An Inquiry into the Condition of Victimhood*, trans. R. Gomme, Princeton: Princeton University Press.

Hirsch, M. (2012), *The Generation of Postmemory: Writing and Visual Culture after the Holocaust*, New York: Columbia University Press.

Hirsch, M. and L. Spitzer (2009), 'The Witness in the Archive: Holocaust Studies/ Memory Studies', *Memory Studies*, 2 (2): 151–70.

Kaplan, E. A. (2016), *Climate Trauma: Foreseeing the Future in Dystopian Film and Fiction*, New Brunswick and New Jersey: Rutgers University Press.

Wieviorka, A. (2006), *The Era of Witness*, trans. J. Stark, Ithaca: Cornell University Press.

Memory and History

Hodgkin, K. and S. Radstone (eds.) (2003), *Contested Pasts: The Politics of Memory*, New York and London: Routledge.

Nora, P. (1989), 'Between Memory and History: Les lieux de mémoire', *Representations*, 26 (7): 24.

Traverso, E. (2016), *Left-Wing Melancholia: Marxism, History, and Memory*, New York: Columbia University Press.

Trouillot, M.-R. (1995), *Silencing the Past: Power and the Production of History*, Boston: Beacon Press.

Transnational Memory Studies

Bond, L. and J. Rapson (eds.) (2014), *The Transcultural Turn : Interrogating Memory between and beyond Borders, Media and Cultural Memory*, Berlin: De Gruyter.

Erll, A. and A. Rigney (eds.) (2018), 'Cultural Memory Studies after the Transnational Turn', *Memory Studies*, 11 (3): 272–385.

Karaca, B., J. Howard, M. Hirsch, M. J. Contreras, A. G. Altınay, and A. Solomon (eds.) (2019), *Women Mobilizing Memory*, New York: Columbia University Press.

Rothberg, M. (2009), *Multidirectional Memory: Remembering the Holocaust in the Age of Decolonization*, Stanford: Stanford University Press.